DEEPER LEARNING

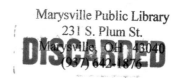
DEEPER LEARNING

HOW EIGHT INNOVATIVE PUBLIC SCHOOLS ARE TRANSFORMING EDUCATION IN THE TWENTY-FIRST CENTURY

MONICA R. MARTINEZ AND DENNIS McGRATH

THE NEW PRESS

NEW YORK
LONDON

© 2014 by Monica R. Martinez and Dennis McGrath
All rights reserved.
No part of this book may be reproduced, in any form, without written permission from the publisher.

Requests for permission to reproduce selections from this book should be mailed to: Permissions Department, The New Press, 120 Wall Street, 31st floor, New York, NY 10005.

Katherine Ellison, author of *Square Peg: My Story and What It Means for Raising Innovators, Visionaries, and Out-of-the-Box Thinkers*, assisted in the writing and editing of this book.

Published in the United States by The New Press, New York, 2014
Distributed by Perseus Distribution

ISBN 978-1-59558-959-0 (hc.)
ISBN 978-1-59558-994-1 (e-book)

CIP data available.

The New Press publishes books that promote and enrich public discussion and understanding of the issues vital to our democracy and to a more equitable world. These books are made possible by the enthusiasm of our readers; the support of a committed group of donors, large and small; the collaboration of our many partners in the independent media and the not-for-profit sector; booksellers, who often hand-sell New Press books; librarians; and above all by our authors.

www.thenewpress.com

Book design and composition by Bookbright Media
This book was set in Adobe Garamond

Printed in the United States of America

10 9 8 7 6 5 4 3 2 1

CONTENTS

DEEPER LEARNING

INTRODUCTION

HOPE: EIGHT REASONS FOR OPTIMISM ABOUT THE FUTURE OF PUBLIC EDUCATION

"Most policymakers—and many school administrators—
have absolutely no idea what kind of instruction is required
to produce students who can think critically and creatively,
communicate effectively, and collaborate versus merely
score well on a test. They are also clueless about what kind
of teaching best motivates this generation to learn. . . . We
need more profiles of quality instruction . . . to inform the
education debate."—Tony Wagner, *Creating Innovators: The
Making of Young People Who Will Change the World*

STATIC SCHOOLS IN A CHANGING WORLD

*In his classic 1968 study of daily life in classrooms, Philip W.
Jackson wrote that students spend as much as 50 percent of their
time waiting for something to happen.[1] They wait for teachers to pass out papers. They wait for slower students to get their
questions answered. They wait for the lunch bell to ring. Alas,
forty-five years after Jackson first published his book, millions of*

American students are still waiting. They're waiting for all of the old reasons, and one relatively new one: today, they're also waiting for our education system to catch up with their lives.

While much of society has changed radically in the twenty-first century, the vast majority of the U.S. public school system—encompassing approximately 133,000 individual schools—still clings to early twentieth-century practices. Teachers lecture while standing in front of rows of desks, students take notes with pencils and lug heavy books, and both groups expect students to memorize content more often than to learn or practice new skills. In general, students are trained to act as followers, not leaders. It's almost as if the digital age—and the attendant changes to the world that came with it—had never happened. Until, of course, it's time to venture beyond school walls. At that point, far too many of them find out they're unprepared.

TIME FOR A CHANGE

Throughout the United States, several million middle and high school students are caught in the disconnect of living in a twenty-first century world while attending twentieth-century secondary schools. These "digital natives" have grown up in a time when communication is instant, memory is outsourced, and job security is a story told by old fogeys—and yet their schools remain focused on preparing them for futures more relevant to days gone by. As the Harvard-based thought leader Tony Wagner warns, today's world doesn't just care about what you know, but what you do with what you know.[2] That new world, in other words, is demanding that digital age workers have digital age skills, including the abilities to think critically, collaborate, and work independently. To date, however, relatively few U.S. secondary schools are designed with these skills in mind.

Wagner and other education experts argue that fixing this problem will require a wholesale transformation of secondary education as we know it. Today's students need much less passive rule following and rote memorization, and much more guidance and support in becoming self-directed learners who are able to take initiative and apply what they learn to a variety of different situations. Above all, they need better preparation to be engaged citizens who survive and thrive in college and in their careers.

As this vision of change has gained clarity and adherents, several names for the shared goals have emerged. Some speak of "college and career readiness." Others refer to "twenty-first-century skills." Still others have adopted phrases including "cognitive and noncognitive skills," "linked learning," and "higher-order thinking."

The expression we like best is a simple one: "Deeper Learning." We chose it not only for its simplicity, but because it fully encompasses the educational goals that, taken together, constitute the foundation for developing the single most important ability students should possess: the capacity for learning how to learn. In an ever-changing world—one in which knowledge and its applications have the potential to shift almost daily—nothing is more valuable.

More specifically, Deeper Learning is the process of preparing and empowering students to master essential academic content, think critically and solve complex problems, work collaboratively, communicate effectively, have an academic mindset, and be self-directed in their education.[3] While all of these are vital components of Deeper Learning, we cannot emphasize enough the importance of the final element on this list: self-direction. Students who are empowered to be the leaders of their own educational lives are capable of embodying a desire to learn unmatched by any that could be instilled by a parent or teacher.

Already there are some five hundred schools in the United States that embrace varying strategies for achieving these ends. Some incorporate ideas that have been influencing parts of school systems for many decades, including practices referred to today as "inquiry-based" and "project-based" learning,[4] and others choose approaches of more recent origin, such as novel ways to integrate cutting-edge information technologies.

The ambitions behind Deeper Learning—primarily to create more independent, self-directed thinkers, better prepared to cope with the modern demands of college, the work force, and the world at large—are broadly popular. Nonetheless, the schools that have truly managed to exemplify them still represent a tiny minority of the American education system at a time when the need for bold change is ever more urgent.

A NATION AT RISK?

With the intention of avoiding unproductive finger-pointing, it's important to note that this Deeper Learning movement is emerging at a time of profound concern on the part of innumerable stakeholders—parents, advocates, educators, and countless others—that a great many U.S. schools are failing our youth and that decades of attempts to fix the problem have in many ways made it worse. In 2009, Elizabeth Coleman, then president of Bennington College, went so far as to charge that American schools are setting students up for "learned helplessness."[5]

To be sure, complaints about the state of schools are nothing new. Both smart and baseless criticisms and reforms date as far back as the 1820s, and some critics charge that today's calls of "crisis" are dangerously overblown.[6] In 1983, just as American high school graduates were on the verge of dazzling the world by creating entirely new industries of computers and software, a presidential commission warned that substandard public education had led to "A Nation at Risk." In an infamous report bearing that cautionary title, the commission wrote: "Our once unchallenged preeminence in commerce, industry, science, and technological innovation is being overtaken by competitors throughout the world."[7]

This fear bolstered the Accountability Movement of the 1990s that was followed by the No Child Left Behind Act of 2001, which increased the focus on standardized testing and low-performing schools. Eight years later came the $4.35 billion Race to the Top initiative, the signature education effort of the Barack Obama administration, which called for comprehensive education reform through the promise of more support for new and better innovations with regard to standards, teacher quality, data systems, and turning around struggling schools.[8]

Despite all of these efforts, fresh evidence has surfaced in the wake of the Great Recession that U.S. students' performance on tests is still lagging behind that of students in other industrialized nations. The United States recently ranked twenty-fourth out of thirty-four nations in "mathematics literacy," and eleventh in "reading literacy."[9] A survey of the class of 2013 found that only 38 percent of high school students were "proficient or above" in reading, with only 26 percent meeting that level for math.[10] And while on average GPAs are rising, SAT scores are falling.[11]

America, which once led the world in the percentage of high school graduates, today ranks twelfth among industrialized nations with regard to high school graduation rates. More than a quarter of U.S. students (more than 1.2 million a year) do not graduate from high school in four years, and for African American and Latino students that number approaches 40 percent. And whereas two generations ago the United States ranked third among industrialized nations in college graduation rates, today with 43 percent we rank twelfth among thirty-seven OECD (Organisation for Economic Co-operation and Development) and G20 (Group of Twenty) nations in the percentage of twenty-five- to thirty-four-year-olds having attained higher education. To underscore the implications of educational attainment on everyday life, in 2011, adults (ages twenty-five to sixty-four) in the United States with a college degree earned on average 77 percent more than those in the same age group who had only a high school degree.[12]

In addition, in survey after survey, U.S. business leaders complain that the majority of job applicants are ill-equipped to solve complex problems, communicate effectively, or work in teams. When four hundred employers were surveyed for a recent major study on work readiness, nearly half of those who hire young people straight from high school said their overall preparation was "deficient."[13] Indeed, as our globalized, digital age economy demands increasingly sophisticated critical thinkers, the gap between high school graduates' abilities and the economy's demands seems to be growing. As Tony Wagner argues, such developments indicate that our schools—even those that score best on standardized tests—aren't failing, but rather are obsolete. This, he writes, presents society with "a very different problem requiring an altogether different solution."

COMMON CORE

Here we will pause, taking a moment to understand how the most recent sea change to the educational landscape fits into the larger picture. The shift has come not in the form of a federal mandate, but rather with the development of the Common Core State Standards (CCSS)—the newest and most sweeping of all the reform efforts to gain traction over the past several decades. To date, forty-five states, representing approximately 80 percent of the K–12 student population, have signed on to the effort, which in sum aspires to make education more rigorous by holding students and teachers to a higher bar. In many states the push for new standards evoked a fervent backlash by parents, teachers, and politicians, who fear it will aggravate what the *New York Times* has called a "testing mania,"[14] and who are legitimately struggling to grasp *how* to implement the requisite changes. For example, Kentucky, a state that has long struggled with the associated challenges of widespread rural poverty, became the first state to adopt the new standards in 2010. Teachers were nothing short of overwhelmed as "overnight, the Pythagorean theorem went from a 10th-grade lesson to an eighth-grade lesson.

Instead of just identifying the first-person point of view, middle-school students suddenly had to be able to explain why an author chose to use it and how that decision influenced the text." Educators and parents were frustrated and concerned that the standards were too high and would simply set students up for failure.[15]

As always, the adjoining politics are complicated. Tea Partiers and others on the right continuously mischaracterize the CCSS, using them as ammunition to demonize the Obama administration. From the left come complaints about the standards being part and parcel of harmful corporate reforms that work to put teachers in the crosshairs. These polarized politics—a hyper-focus on testing debates by traditional progressives on one hand and on the other, reductive, oversimplified, and even false claims by conservatives—are having an unfortunate, if not dire, effect on a vital opportunity to improve education for the mass of American students.

The CCSS represent a historic opening to usher in a new mode of learning that reflects the times in which we live and puts at the center of education the goal of teaching for deep understanding. Yet, as Randi Weingarten, president of the American Federation of Teachers, puts it, "Even good ideas can be torpedoed by bad execution."[16] Getting the CCSS right is essential. One of the many reasons we wrote this book is to show how to "get it right" through examples of schools that have been doing just that (and more), well before these recent debates took hold. Why do we have to get it right? Because if we do, in fact, want kids—particularly underserved students—to be college and career ready and equipped to take on the myriad challenges of the future, we have no choice.

The question is: What does getting it right actually look like? The CCSS, in their current iteration, do come up short on indispensable tenets that we have taken care to highlight in this book—namely by a failure to address the importance of self-direction, collaboration, and effective communication—but nevertheless they are designed specifically to develop critical thinking and problem-solving skills, and mastery of essential knowledge.

We mentioned Kentucky previously. As one of the first states to get on the CCSS bandwagon, in many ways it can help other states avoid fatal missteps. It is each state's responsibility to ensure that schools and teachers have the tools, guidance, and resources that are necessary to support and prepare students to meet the new standards. No small charge, but this is what must happen. And as happened with the rollout of the standards in Kentucky, parents and families need to be educated and informed about the what, why, and how of it all. This movement to transform education in America cannot simply amount to raising a bar that students can never reach; it can and should move teaching and learning toward the practices that, as years of research and evidence have shown, create adaptive, lifelong learners.

The challenges to implementing the CCSS are large and very real, but let's not throw out the baby with the bathwater. Rather than fixate or complain, let's strategize about, contribute to, and rally for tangible improvements to the entire process. We need real, ongoing support for schools and teachers implementing the CCSS, better assessments intended to measure learning (which require a great deal of thoughtful craftsmanship), and quality resources for understanding the ways in which essential skills are developed in students. Our hope is that this book—a display of Deeper Learning in action—can serve as a resource for transforming secondary education, making it possible for our nation to embrace this chance at real change. Higher standards are but one way, albeit an important one, of signaling that we as a nation believe that all of our young people deserve better.

So the Tea Party is wrong, and the progressives are wrong. Common Core is in fact *at* the core of the most important equity issue of our times. If done right, by being broadened in scope and supported, not simply mandated, all kids—rather than being tracked into educational mirrors of society's social stratification as they have been for decades—will have the knowledge and skills they need. Our country desperately needs a way forward to achieve both equity in our schools and better outcomes for every student.

A BETTER WAY

In the early 1980s, on the heels of the flare sent up by "A Nation at Risk," Theodore R. Sizer published his seminal treatise on high school in America, *Horace's Compromise: The Dilemma of the American High School*.[17] Yet much of the wisdom set forth in his work about how to transform the experience of secondary school failed to take center stage amid the urgent cries and ensuing wave of responses unleashed by the aforementioned infamous report. In terms of reform, the time has come for the long view—a marriage, of sorts, between Sizer's vision and the latest efforts to respond to our expanding educational crises.

By now, you may already have guessed at our choice for a solution. In two words, it's Deeper Learning. Because we want high schools, parents, and policymakers to better understand the breadth of what that actually means, and because we agree with Wagner and other education innovators that all of us need more and better ideas of what quality teaching and learning looks like, the two of us set out, beginning in 2011, to find a sample of secondary schools that exemplify Deeper Learning principles. Our hope is that this book will ramp up efforts to implement these ideas and principles, and help provide a bridge to the future.

We tapped our networks to narrow down a field of several U.S. schools with reputations for helping students pursue Deeper Learning objectives, whether or not they called them by that name. We then further pared down the list by seeking geographical diversity, including secondary schools from both coasts and the Midwest, as well as from both rural and urban communities. We also took care to choose institutions serving high percentages of minority and low-income students to drive home the point that while Deeper Learning will look different from one school to the next, its core values can be embraced in a range of environments and adapted to a school's specific circumstances. Through our sample of schools, we hope to create a space for readers to be inspired and believe that the schools in their communities—be they urban, suburban, rural, affluent, struggling, or middle income—can transform in similarly innovative ways. Our purpose here is to show that the rich experiences and the foundation for success offered through Deeper Learning can and should be afforded to *all* students. In particular, students facing economic challenges in a world where race still matters may stand to gain even more from the empowering strategies we'll detail.

After settling on a group of finalists, we conducted telephone interviews with the principals of each candidate school, evaluating them across each Deeper Learning objective and also according to their focus on integrating technology. Finally, we chose eight secondary schools that we believe are particularly inspiring models. From 2011–12, the two of us visited the schools for several days each to observe and interview teachers, students, and principals, with the goal of presenting a vivid, on-the-ground view of what transformative education looks like.[18]

It's an opportune moment, as teachers and principals throughout America begin to adopt Common Core curricula. As mentioned above, this change has provoked great controversy, less to do with the Common Core *ideals*, but rather the question of how teachers can achieve them. Most of the schools we visited have already transitioned to the CCSS. Their leaders believe, as we do, that Deeper Learning principles chart the most efficacious path not only to integrate new curricula, but to support an even more holistic development of every student's potential and create a new kind of student: a self-directed leader of his or her own educational career who succeeds in higher education and beyond.

The schools we selected are:

Avalon School, a charter school serving seventh through twelfth graders in St. Paul, Minnesota;

Casco Bay High School and **King Middle School** in Portland, Maine;

High Tech High, the flagship in a charter network of two elementary schools, four middle schools, and five high schools in San Diego, California;

Impact Academy of Arts & Technology, a charter high school in Hayward, California;

MC² STEM High School in Cleveland, Ohio;

Rochester High School, the only district high school in Rochester, Indiana; and

Science Leadership Academy, a magnet STEM (science, technology, engineering, and mathematics) high school in Philadelphia, Pennsylvania.

All eight of these schools are public, including the one magnet school, Science Leadership Academy, and the charters: Avalon School, High Tech High, and Impact Academy. When we visited the Avalon School, 32 percent of the students were eligible to receive free and reduced-price lunches, the lowest proportion of any of the schools. At the other schools, that percentage ranged between 45 and 100 percent. Minority enrollment was more than 30 percent in seven of the eight schools, and more than 60 percent in four of them. (Rochester High, in rural Indiana, is the exception, with a minority student population of only 8 percent, which is typical of the region. It is worth noting that the number of students at Rochester qualifying for free and reduced-price lunches has been steadily increasing in recent years. This is a constituency that we believe is important to represent.)

The institutions we selected were slightly smaller than
the norm for U.S. secondary schools. All have fewer than
600 students, compared to the national average enrollment
of about 693.[19] The smallest of the eight, the Avalon School,
served 185 students at the time we visited. Nonetheless, as
we intend to show, most if not all of their effective strategies
could be adopted in larger schools.

The majority of the schools we selected are relatively new in
one way or another, having opened or transformed their design and approach within the past twelve years. Nonetheless,
many have already achieved some measure of public distinc-
tion or recognition. *Business Week* magazine named the Avalon
School one of Minnesota's top five high schools. Edutopia.org
lauded Casco Bay High School and MC^2. High Tech High
has been celebrated in numerous articles and books due to its
innovative tactics and high graduation rates. By the school's
data reports, 98 percent of High Tech High graduates go on
to college, while more than 30 percent enter math or science
fields. King Middle School, widely praised along with Casco
Bay as one of the top schools in Maine, has been profiled on
the *PBS NewsHour*, and *Ladies' Home Journal* named Science
Leadership Academy one of "The Ten Most Amazing Schools
in the U.S."[20]

What all of our schools have in common is that they are
reimagining how teachers teach and students learn. In each
of them, teachers collaborate far more than the norm, supporting each other and jointly taking responsibility for the
students' success. In each, as well, the bottom-line goal is to
help students become more engaged in and responsible for
their own learning. Their formulas appear to be working, as
they have achieved both higher graduation rates and higher

percentages of college admissions than the average rates for the districts and states in which they are located.

We're convinced that the eight schools we profile on the pages to come are showcases of ways to prepare students for today's world by creating engaged, collaborative, creative, and self-directed critical thinkers. As we discovered on our visits, they meet these goals with a set of common strategies listed here and examined more fully in the chapters to come.

All of the schools:

- Establish cohesive, collaborative learning communities that sharply differ from the top-down national norm;

- Empower and encourage students to become more self-directed, creative, and cooperative by getting them out of their chairs and more directly involved in their own education;

- Make curricula more engaging, memorable, and meaningful by integrating subjects and establishing relevance to real-world concerns;

- Reach outside classroom walls to extend the idea and purpose of learning beyond school, forming partnerships with businesses, organizations, research institutions, and colleges and universities;

- Inspire students by endeavoring to understand their talents and interests, customizing learning whenever possible to discover the motivational "hook" for each young person; and

- Incorporate technology purposefully to enhance, rather than simply automate, learning.

GOING DEEPER

Once again, not all of the teachers and principals we interviewed used the phrase Deeper Learning to describe the outcomes they were seeking. Yet all embraced the specific Deeper Learning goals of students mastering core academic content, thinking critically and solving complex problems, working collaboratively, communicating effectively, and being self-directed learners with an academic mindset.

Despite widespread support, those espousing Deeper Learning principles have their critics, some of whom interpret the priorities as a call to jettison time-honored academic content, tests, and rigor for a loosey-goosey, touchy-feely ethic. For example, in a May 2013 blog, Tom Loveless, a Senior Fellow at the Brookings Institution and one of the most vehement critics of the push to spread these approaches, dismissed Deeper Learning by name as the latest "anti-knowledge" fad, grouping it with initiatives for "project-based learning, inquiry and discovery learning, higher-level thinking, critical thinking, outcome-based education, and 21st Century skills." Not only do these movements lack evidence to support their claims, he argued, but they also exacerbate social inequality. "If public schools don't teach algebra or chemistry or history or great literature or how to write well—the old-fashioned learning that has been around for centuries and remains high status knowledge in most cultures—rich kids will get it somewhere else," Loveless wrote. "Poor kids won't."[21]

This view seriously misinterprets Deeper Learning's methods and intentions. Our eight schools, along with hundreds of others throughout the nation, are anything but anti-knowledge. Not a single one of them is ready to trade a solid foundation in science and literature for new-age jargon and feel-good classroom exercises, as some may associate with older varieties of "alternative" schools. They want to change the current, conventional method of teaching from what the celebrated learning expert Sir Ken Robinson describes as "a delivery system" to a more dynamic teacher role of mentoring, stimulating, provoking, and engaging students to acquire skills that in turn will help them most efficiently to gain knowledge[22] and go on to become lifetime learners. Among the list of Deeper Learning objectives is the aspiration to know and master core academic content. Deeper Learning adherents simply believe that achieving that goal requires students to develop a sense of responsibility for their own learning and that in order for that to happen, they must be motivated and engaged. Some have termed it "progressive education 2.0." While we find this slightly reductive, it does make the point that Deeper Learning looks quite different from most of what has become familiar on either end of the education spectrum.

Evidence backing up an education based on Deeper Learning principles continues to build, however; early support—the kind of evidence that critics such as Loveless say is lacking—came in a 2008 study[23] of seven hundred California students in three high schools, two of which had large proportions of minority and English-language learner students, while the third served mostly white, high-income students. At the start of the study, one of the more diverse schools redesigned its algebra and geometry programs according to Deeper Learning guidelines, coaching students on how to ask good questions and assess themselves and the group. Initially, incoming ninth graders at that school were performing significantly below those at the other schools in

math, but by the end of that first year they had caught up
with their peers in algebra, and by the next year they were
performing significantly better than students in the other two
schools. By the fourth year of the study, 41 percent of the students exposed to Deeper Learning strategies were taking calculus, compared to just 27 percent at the other two schools.

While such reports are impressive, they don't come close to
telling the full story of what schools like the eight we selected
have to offer their students and the greater public. In our
modern society, it's becoming ever clearer that small groups
of collaborators will produce the products and ideas that create growth and jobs and improve the world in countless other
ways. These schools are training students in the skills they
need to do just that. More broadly, by supporting teachers in
helping students acquire a love of learning, these schools are
inspiring personal transformations, motivating students to acquire a learning lifestyle that will follow them on to college
and throughout their lives.

In the following pages, you'll hear directly from the teachers who work to make it all possible. In Portland, Maine, Gus
Goodwin gives eighth graders at King Middle School a visceral understanding of electricity as they design and build
small wind turbines, while national award-winning English
teacher Susan McCray uses what she learned leading wil-
derness adventure trips to immerse Casco Bay High School
students in the lives of homeless residents of Appalachia. At
Rochester High in Indiana, science teacher Amy Blackburn
inspires ninth graders to brainstorm ways to improve efficiency at the local hospital's emergency room—and present
their ideas to the hospital nurses. And in Cleveland, Ohio,
Brian McCalla, who surrendered a world-traveling job to

teach, infects students at MC^2 STEM High School with his zeal for industrial design. These talented, passionate professionals thrive in cultures that give them unusual autonomy, logistical support, and opportunities for collaboration, and the fruit of their labors is evident.

As Chris Lehmann, principal of Science Leadership Academy, describes it, schools like his strive to help students become "the best versions of themselves." During our visits, we repeatedly found evidence of how well they are succeeding.

You'll also hear about students including Andrea Lane, a math whiz who was bored and distracted in middle school, but who flourished at MC^2 in Cleveland after discovering a love of engineering. Holly Marsh got "hooked" on her career path by studying ecology at the Avalon School in St. Paul, going on to spend more than three hundred hours volunteering at a national park, where she was hired as a park ranger the day before her sixteenth birthday. Justin Ehringhaus was a shy, average student at Casco Bay High School, in Portland, Maine, before his teachers egged him on to follow his curiosity about Asia, a path that led him to live and study in Japan and China.

What can't be discounted is that in each case, the remarkable schools we profile in this book have helped young men and women not only to acquire learning skills they can use throughout their lives, but to tap the connections that have changed education from being a duty to a passion. "I fell in love with a place that I first hated with my heart and soul," Casco Bay graduating senior Abde Ahmed told his classmates and teachers at an end-of-year ceremony. A Sudanese immigrant, Ahmed had evolved from a skeptical sophomore to a gung-ho junior and senior, according to his teachers. He explained that metamorphosis to his fellow students and teachers: "I fell in love because of you. Because of all of you." Schools in all sorts of communities throughout the country can and should transform into similarly inspiring centers of learning.

A BLUEPRINT FOR DEEPER LEARNING

While we're not fans of rote memorization, we thought it might be useful to end each chapter with a few distilled points in the hopes that it will help readers retain the information. With that goal, here are four key takeaways from what you've read so far:

- The majority of today's schools don't reflect the tremendous changes and new demands that characterize American society and shape life in the digital age.

- Deeper Learning—a more robust and responsive educational experience—offers a framework for educators and schools to rise to the challenge of preparing students for college, careers, and the world today.

- This book showcases Deeper Learning through eight schools that have taken on the challenge of adapting to the needs of students today. They are educating students—from a range of backgrounds—to develop the skills they'll most need to reach their full potential in the twenty-first century.

- A critical objective of Deeper Learning is for students to become more responsible for their own education, something the teachers and principals at our eight schools make possible through embracing six core strategies: create a cohesive, genuinely collaborative school environment; make learning more active and engaging; integrate subjects with each other and with real-world issues; reach beyond school walls to make learning meaningful by involving partners in the wider community; inspire students by finding the "hooks" that motivate them; and incorporate technology in ways that enrich and support learning experiences.

1

CONNECT

CREATE A COMMUNITY OF LEARNERS

"There is only one of me. You need to look to each other."—Gus Goodwin, education technology teacher at King Middle School

"I MIGHT FIT INTO THIS SCHOOL"

The first surprise for students on their first day at the Avalon Charter School in St. Paul, Minnesota, is visual. The one-story, red-brick former warehouse, in the middle of an urban industrial park, looks more like an office building than a traditional high school campus. Youth are assigned their own mini cubicles instead of lockers, and classrooms are separated by glass walls. The chairs are set in circles instead of rows.

More surprises come when the teachers start to talk. They refer to themselves not as teachers but advisors, and introduce the nervous new ninth graders to junior and senior students who, in a sharp departure from conventional schools, seem eager to behave like mentors rather than predators.

For most of the new students, however, the biggest surprise of the first school day comes when their new advisors ask two entirely unfamiliar questions: "What do you want to learn?" and "What would you like to do better?" Year after year, at this juncture in Project Brainstorm, Avalon's orientation routine, the new students stare back with open mouths. Some mumble, "I don't know!"

"There's always this blankness," says social studies teacher Carrie Bakken. "I don't think many of them, if any of them, have ever been asked those questions." Bakken, whose straight, ash-blonde hair and youthful face make her look like a student herself, is a refugee from law school who discovered her passion for teaching after a class in juvenile justice made her realize she'd rather try to help kids before they wound up in the system. She often steps in at this point.

"What do you do when nobody tells you what you should be doing?" she'll ask. "Even if they say 'I like to play video games,' that's okay for now. It's a way to jump-start the process. They can end up doing a project on video games that can still teach them how to find good sources and turn in quality research."

On our visit to Avalon, we saw Project Brainstorm in action. Once the students got over their initial shock at being asked what they wanted to learn, they wrote lists on yellow Post-its, which the teachers directed them to stick on to a long sheet of paper that subsequently was hung on a nearby wall. Several students wanted to learn a foreign language—one said she wanted to learn sign language. Several others, as Bakken had anticipated, wanted to play video games; a few asked to work in the school's garden, and one wanted to know how a nuclear reactor works.

Then came a new challenge, as Nora Whalen, who teaches American history, asked another pair of unfamiliar questions: "What are you good at?" and "What do you know?"

Eyes widened and mouths fell open, just as Whalen and Bakken had told us they always do.

"You can talk about being good at anything," Whalen coaxed. "It doesn't have to be something academic." She herself, she said, knew how to change a diaper.

This time, blue Post-its covered a new white sheet, with students listing skills such as playing the guitar, sketching, and speaking Russian.

Whalen addressed the group again, pointing to the wall. "This sheet shows everything you all want to learn," she said, and, pointing again, "This sheet shows what everyone has to offer to the group. You all have signed your Post-it notes, so you can now identify someone who can be a resource for what you want to learn. The staff can't teach you all the things you want to know. We are not the only experts in the room . . . you need to connect with one another to expand your learning."

For the rest of the school year, the two Post-it–covered sheets would be kept on a wall in the main entryway, reminding students both of the many interests that motivate learning and of the benefits available by looking to each other for support.

At the end of Project Brainstorm, after several more exercises of this sort, students sat in a circle and wrote down their first impressions of their new school on index cards, which they threw into the center of the circle for others to pick up and read aloud.

Not every comment was sanguine. "I cannot wait to graduate," said one. But most were.

"The feeling of this school is awesome," one student wrote.

"I might fit into this school," penned another.

"Today wasn't as dumb as I thought it was going to be," wrote a third.

BEYOND SPIRIT RALLIES

In Philip Jackson's aforementioned book on life in the classroom, he likened American K–12 schools to prisons and mental institutions, since both attendance and obedience are required in all three. However, teachers in today's most forward-thinking schools work determinedly to end such comparisons and instead create a dynamic vision of what institutions designed for learning can look like. Traditionally, building community in schools invokes images of rallying around an athletic team, or perhaps a political or social cause. Indeed, this type of community building has its benefits. Yet in more academic terms, what does it mean to create community around learning and, more specifically, build a learning community that is actually driven by the learners and skillfully maintained by teachers and other professionals?

Avalon and the other schools we highlight hold fast to the belief that developing students into self-directed, responsible learners concerned for the learning of others is a fundamental requirement for Deeper Learning. But helping students become responsible for their own learning is an incredibly challenging task that cannot be accomplished by any individual teacher acting alone. What is demonstrated vividly through Avalon and the other schools is the power of a learning community to transform students' lives when a culture exists that values relationships, trust, and respect, and simultaneously presses students consistently to do their best—by the setting of high expectations, and the support and encouragement needed to meet them—through a collective responsibility for learning. Blending and balancing all of these aspects is where many schools swing too far in one direction or another.

Schools should be consciously designed so that these elements feed each other and none falls by the wayside.

At most schools, particularly secondary schools, it's much more common for parents and teachers than it is for students to care about whether learning is actually happening. It's anything but easy to motivate a teenager trained by years of passive education to express his interests, much less pursue them, as several teachers reminded us. Fortunately, considerable research shows that schools can raise teens' enthusiasm for learning in ways that begin with creating strong communities.[1] Back in 1993, a study by the researcher Anthony S. Bryk, who later became president of the Carnegie Foundation for the Advancement of Teaching, found that a combination of supportive social relationships and strong emphasis on academics contributed to the remarkable success that urban Catholic schools were engendering among economically disadvantaged students.[2] As Bryk later suggested, based on a longitudinal study of four hundred schools in the city of Chicago, academic achievement is strongly correlated with students' experience of trust. "Absent such trust, schools find it nearly impossible to strengthen parent-community ties, build professional capacity, and enable a student-centered learning climate."[3] This wasn't to say that trust in itself guarantees success, but rather that schools with little or no trust were unlikely to improve.

The type of foundation we're describing is especially important when it comes to students developing what are commonly referred to as twenty-first-century skills. The task requires hard work and personal commitment, which students offer much more willingly when they feel positively about their teachers and each other, and believe they belong to a mission-driven team. "If you want to teach well to very high standards, you have to know the students well, and you have to have that relationship that allows you to both challenge them, and adapt what you're doing for them so that it works,"[4] Linda Darling-Hammond, Stanford University's Charles E. Ducommun Professor of Education, noted in a PBS interview.

Positive social ties and continual reminders of adults' high expectations contribute to what educational researcher Camille A. Farrington has dubbed an "academic mindset." In a 2013 review of several studies, Farrington found that motivation to pursue Deeper Learning objectives depends on four key perceptions by students: "I belong to this academic community"; "I can succeed at this"; "My ability and competence grows with my effort"; and "This work has value for me."[5] We found schools pressing home these messages in a variety of ways, as teachers constantly called on students to identify their interests, ask questions, solve problems, analyze, communicate, collaborate with one another, and seek out resources and opportunities to enrich and expand their learning.

The teachers and school leaders we observed accomplished these feats by creating close-knit, supportive school communities where high expectations for the type of learning that will take place are held by students and educators alike. The strategies they use combine disorienting self-directed exercises, such as Avalon's Project Brainstorm; a heavy emphasis on trust; atypical physical environments; regular, formal, and conspicuous reminders of the community's aspirations and norms; and an extraordinary amount of autonomy and cooperation, for both teachers and students. These tactics take a lot more thought and planning than your standard spirit rallies, and they certainly do much more than create a feel-good atmosphere.

While the precise texture of every successful learning community varies, each of our schools concedes that students having solid, meaningful connections to teachers, other students, and to the experience of learning are preconditions for true academic rigor. To boot, the byproducts of trusting, learning-centered communities—safer, more nurturing schools—offer important insight for developing solutions to persistent challenges around behavior and discipline. Creating an atmosphere that reinforces the notion of students taking responsibility for both their own learning and for the learning of their peers—a cornerstone of these strong communities— has a broad, positive impact on how students and teachers generally conduct themselves—derived from their empowered roles in school. All of this results in something very different from the "schooling" that continues to prevail in classrooms throughout the country today. Deeper Learning happens when schools build from the idea that everyone is in it together.

DIS-ORIENTATION RITUALS

To create strong communities of self-directed learners, teachers and principals told us they often need to actively disrupt students' expectations, making a clean break with histories of passive, rote learning practices that often leave students in a solitary place, disconnected from the learning experiences of other students. As with Avalon's Project Brainstorm, many schools accomplish this task with what we've come to think of as *dis*-orientation rituals. A common recurring feature of these efforts to set new norms is a strong focus on shaping a mentoring relationship between upper-class members (students in upper grade levels) and younger or new students. The impact of tackling that age-old tradition of older students tormenting those new on the block is striking.

At Science Leadership Academy, new students plunge into unfamiliar, project-based learning during an extraordinary orientation week called Summer Institute. Assigned to small groups, they head out to conduct research in downtown Philadelphia, formulating questions, collecting facts, and making observations about the public library, train station, and park, and then working together on presentations to creatively report their findings using mediums from PowerPoint slides to theatrical scripts. The exercise spans several days, during which students receive only occasional coaching from their new teachers and a few upper-class members assigned as guides, while the newcomers become viscerally familiar with the school's core values of inquiry, research, collaboration, presentation, and reflection.

At MC² STEM High School, current students plan and run the new-student orientation program, called Activation Week. Seniors take responsibility for the first day of the week, while the sophomores and juniors assist with the second day. MC² English teacher Fee Mackinnon notes: "We try to communicate to all the students who help out that they are a vital part of what we are trying to do, and that they will be modeling what we want to instill in the ninth graders."

The older students proudly explain the school's culture, traditions, and language to the newcomers, whom they understand may be feeling overwhelmed. There's a lot that's new and different from the new students' past experience, including, in particular, the MC^2 practice of "mastery learning," which means that rather than getting letter grades, the students' projects are rated as "exceeding mastery, mastery, reaching mastery, and basic." The sophomores and juniors, whose task it is to explain this to the younger students, try to make the process as concrete as possible by reviewing a typical report card.

Of all the dis-orientation rituals we learned of, the freshman "quest" at Casco Bay High School in Portland, Maine, was particularly ambitious. For three days, incoming ninth graders and their teachers camp out in yurts on a nearby island, where they kayak, hike, and cook meals together, while simultaneously embarking on a unit studying the nature of communities, from ecosystems to Masai tribes. Principal Derek Pierce calls the exercise a vital tool to adapt incoming freshmen to the school's culture, which includes a heavy emphasis on field experiences and high academic expectations. "We get students from three different middle schools and some private schools," Pierce told us. "Each year we have to assemble a class community that will help students do things they didn't think they could possibly do."

The ninth-grade quest culminates with a dis-orientation ceremony similar to the one at Avalon, but considerably more challenging for the new students. At an all-school meeting, each freshman must make a presentation to the rest of the students about the kinds of skills and personal experiences he or she will be contributing to the Casco Bay community. At one point, each new student writes down one word or phrase to describe the planned contribution, and places it in a box held by two seniors standing in the front of the room.

"I bring lacrosse skills," read one of the recent notes.

"I bring a kind heart," read another.

"I bring a terrible middle school experience," read a third.

After delivering his or her message, each freshman leaves the room, with only two class members remaining behind. These two formally ask the remaining students whether the school will allow the freshmen class to enter the community.

"Do we accept this box?" the two seniors shouted at the end of one recent ceremony, holding the box of notes over their heads. The room exploded in cheering, and the freshmen returned, looking excited and relieved.

Adding to the emotional power of the quest, each new ninth grader receives a letter of advice written by a senior student while camping out on the island. The content of the letters varies from suggestions about what classes to take to more general encouragements about supporting their peers and trusting their teachers. When the ninth graders return from the island, each freshman is assigned to interview his or her senior mentor to learn more, and then to make a poster that includes a picture of the two of them and a short, reflective essay on what has been learned. The posters hang throughout the school's hallways as ever-present reminders of what the learning experience at Casco Bay is all about.

The modeling taking place through these early rituals is powerful. From the start, through these initiations, incoming students encounter the types of roles they'll have in the school as they interact with more seasoned pupils and bear witness to students taking the lead, helping and guiding one another. Their comfort zones and ideas of how school and learning happen are challenged almost immediately through activities designed to draw out who they are, what they need, and what they can contribute. And the experiences are punctuated by opportunities to form positive ties with other members of the school community, reinforcing the sense that no one is alone on this new educational journey.

A CONNECTED COMMUNITY—TRUST, TIES, AND MENTORS

To better understand why building trusting communities is no frill when it comes to learning, consider what Casco Bay High School English teacher Susan McCray has observed. "One of the reasons that we have the dropout rates that we have in schools is that we have these large monolithic places where people walk through the halls anonymously. And no one notices whether they're there or not. Why would you go someplace where you don't know whether someone's going to notice whether you're there or not?"

Being noticed certainly made all the difference for David Boone, a star graduate of MC^2.[6] Boone was fourteen when his home was destroyed by members of a gang that he had refused to join. He and his mother and siblings had to split up as they shuttled between homes of friends and relatives. As a sophomore at MC^2, Boone spent a few nights sleeping at the school, and other nights sleeping on park benches, which soon came to the attention of his teachers and MC^2's principal, Jeff McClellan.

"This kid was doing everything right," McClellan told us. "He just needed a little support." McClellan and his staff went to great lengths to help Boone weather the challenges of being homeless and to reduce the impact that such stressful circumstances could have on his educational and life outcomes.

Boone, who has since blogged about his experiences for the *Huffington Post*,[7] today credits the support he received—from his relatives, friends, and various school professionals, including McClellan—for the invaluable turn of events that would forever change his life. In the fall of 2012, after being accepted by more than twenty colleges, Boone enrolled at Harvard University, on a full scholarship.

Boone is just one of many students who have benefited from the varying ways a school community can and should offer a network of support. Schools that take care to create trusting communities establish virtuous cycles in which hardy relationships enable a steady focus on learning while discouraging all sorts of negative behavior, including rule breaking and bullying. Teachers consequently spend much less time and energy than their colleagues in less-connected environments on policing and managing behavior and more on helping kids learn, which may help explain the high achievement rates at the schools we visited. The evidence-based relationship between students' emotional states and their ability to learn is beginning to take hold as shown by the recent boom in "social-emotional learning" programs at thousands of K–12 schools throughout America.[8]

The trend makes sense. Consider Abraham. Maslow's famous graphic representation of the hierarchy of human needs. In this pyramid model, a sense of physical safety lies at the broad foundation, right after breathing and eating. Next comes a sense of love and belonging, followed by self-esteem and respect from others. Only at the pyramid's top—i.e., once all of the more basic needs are met—did Maslow believe it possible to pursue the more abstract goals of morality, creativity, spontaneity, and the acquisition of facts.[9]

Alas, most U.S. schools fail to provide even this basic foundation for learning, judged by recent statistics on bullying. National surveys have found that one-third of all U.S. schoolchildren have reported being teased or bullied at school. Researchers have shown that bullying not only creates more anxiety and depression among students[10]—even those who merely witness it—but also significantly hurts academic performance, lowering GPAs and scores on tests.[11]

In recent decades, many anti-bullying programs tested in schools throughout the world have failed to make any difference. Those that espouse a zero tolerance approach, with harsh disciplinary action for the bullies, have been particularly disappointing, tending to reduce the reporting of bullying (by intimidated students) but not the bullying itself. However, research suggests that thoughtful programs that start with creating strong school communities and include social and emotional learning opportunities can indeed make a difference. A study by scientists based in Chicago who examined more than two hundred school-based anti-bullying programs found an average 11 percent gain in performance on achievement tests,[12] suggesting that the ethos promoted through a school's culture—for example, one that explicitly espouses trust and a shared responsibility for all students—can cultivate a more respectful learning environment.

One effective way we saw a sense of trust created from day one is by assigning new students to small, cohesive groups that stick together for most or all of their school careers. At both King Middle School and Casco Bay High School, for instance, new students join "crews" that share the same advisor for the next three to four years. The metaphor, borrowed from Outward Bound programs, is obvious: the students are all in the same boat, and are expected to pull their own weight. "'Crew' means having a support system that will never fail you," said one senior girl at Casco Bay, in a school video. "There's an unspoken understanding that if anything goes wrong, the rest of us are going to be there for you."

Research in recent years has also documented the importance of students feeling connected to adults at their school in terms of their future achievement.[13] A specific method of supporting such trust-based relationships is with an "advisory" period, a kind of homeroom during which students, who are usually in the same group for three to four years, can informally check in with each other and with their same teacher, who follows them through their school career. At Avalon School, for instance, the advisory period lasts just twenty minutes and it's a ritual that students cherish. English teacher Kevin Ward told us, "Advisory is the most powerful thing we do."[14]

To help create trust in the new community, and build that essential foundation for an "academic mindset," teachers commonly recruit upper-class members as models and guides for younger students, as previously described in the innovative orientation practices. "The older kids are really important in socializing the new students," Jeremy Spry, a Science Leadership Academy program coordinator, told us. "They tell their story to the newer kids that this is a great school and that the work they do here is meaningful to them. They also help answer questions and give the new students a sense of what things will be like here."

At Rochester High in Indiana, twelfth graders, referred to

as "critical friends," critique ninth graders' papers to model effective feedback. The freshmen then write reflective essays on what they've learned, and how they might now go about giving good feedback to one another.

This is a powerful teaching tactic, as much research suggests. Beginning in the 1960s, Stanford University's Albert Bandura published seminal studies on the "social learning theory,"[15] according to which, as Bandura and his followers detailed, children learn by observing and imitating influential models, particularly those most similar to them. It's important for schools not only to tap the wealth of knowledge and resources of their teachers but to show that learning—academic or otherwise—can and should happen everywhere, all the time. Student mentoring and guidance is one of the most effective ways to model a more robust perception of the learning process.

At Avalon, teachers encourage new students to seek out older kids' advice, asking questions such as: "If you could do your freshman year over, what would you do differently?" or "What was the best advice you got when you were a freshman?"

Avalon founding teacher Carrie Bakken described how she assigned a transfer student who was getting poor grades to a senior who helped show her the ropes. The transfer student's troubles owed to her unfamiliarity with the school's new routines, including the practice of logging into a computer system all of the hours she spent working on her projects. The senior student recalled how he had been helped with this very problem by an older student three years earlier, and repeated his former mentor's advice that "If you don't log the work you've done every day, you will be a hundred hours behind before you know it." The new student quickly improved, later telling Bakken, "No senior would have ever helped me at my old school. I felt safe knowing I had a partner."

Avalon upper-class members told us that they believe being a mentor is an honor, and many eagerly volunteer to take on the role. In fact, in past years, so many seniors have volunteered to be mentors that teachers had to establish a formal application process. Throughout the year, the teachers work to recognize the student volunteers with activities such as ice cream socials.

In addition to proving effective among students of different ages and skill levels, social learning also works with peers. Through organized peer-to-peer feedback experiences designed to promote self-directed learning and collaboration under the guidance of teachers, students doing similar work can share with each other the learning strategies they've discovered on their own.

We saw this in action at Science Leadership Academy in Philadelphia, where, after a vocabulary quiz, tenth-grade English teacher Larissa Pahomov asked the students who had received a perfect grade to raise their hands. She then told the students who had missed some words to talk to those who hadn't and find out why. (Among the secrets revealed was a free learning tool, featuring virtual flashcards, that a student had found online.)

It's crucial for teachers to continually press the message that students are responsible for each other, and for their shared academic success. At King Middle School, education technology teacher Gus Goodwin explained how he managed a group of eighth graders, who, during a collaborative project, had begun to treat their classmates poorly, ignoring or ridiculing their comments.

First, Goodwin interviewed several students and had others fill out a survey asking what sorts of behavior would contribute to the best school environment. Again and again, the respondents said they wanted to learn and have fun, and that they wanted other students to be respectful and not interrupt or criticize their ideas. Goodwin wrote these responses on a six-by-six-foot chart that he posted in his classroom.

Ever since then, Goodwin has started each new term by giving students a worksheet on which they rate themselves according to five goals: respect, responsibility, empathy, and being an interested learner and an effective communicator. Three or four times a term, he also asks them to write reports in their journals on their progress toward helping to build the school community. A typical entry might be:

Goal: I am going to work on encouraging others.

Reflection: Someone's project was falling apart. I saw this and went over to help them out. In the end the project worked.

By providing a common language and concrete goals, the worksheet, journals, and chart have all helped keep students focused on improving how they engage with expectations that everyone agrees on, Goodwin said. Today, when he spots a student misbehaving in class, he will often walk over and say, "Let's go review the chart," almost as if it were the chart, not Goodwin, expressing disappointment. Standing by the diagram, he'll ask the student to rank his or her conduct according to the listed goals. Then he'll ask: "What's going on?"

With educators playing the role of coach, reminder, and guide, this heightened sense of trust in students to have some ownership over both expectations and actions is at the core of effective learning communities. It evens out the arcane balance of power that adolescents are notoriously resistant to, and underscores that school really is about them—and about learning. Trust also plays a huge part in the ways that schools offer degrees of autonomy to students, cementing the notion that in school and beyond they are the directors of their own educational lives, something we will delve into more later on in this chapter.

Goodwin also repeatedly reminds his students that, given their school's emphasis on collaborative projects, they are ultimately responsible not just for their own achievements, but for those of their classmates. "There is only one of me," he tells them. "You need to look to each other."

IF THESE WALLS COULD TALK

Right alongside working to create a supportive and trusting environment through student connection and relationships, equally important are the messages signaled by the physical environment. If building a connected community focused on Deeper Learning is the goal, the material experience that students encounter on a daily basis should communicate just that.

The main campus of the High Tech High network, for instance, is a 39,000-square-foot former U.S. Navy engineering training center near the San Diego airport. That's a lot of space for four hundred teenagers, and the lofty ceilings, ample light from abundant windows, and 15-foot glass walls separating classrooms all enhance the sense of openness and possibilities, and emphasize the transparency expected of students and staff alike. Using a preferred technique of many Deeper Learning schools, High Tech High eschews the traditional rows of desks in favor of easily movable furniture and even movable walls, which can accommodate both small and large groups. Students immediately understand that they will not be sitting quietly all day listening to lectures, but will instead be involved in active and dynamic experiences.

Somewhat similarly, at SLA, teachers have reconfigured a former school district administration building to encourage a sense of community. Chris Lehmann, the principal, occupies an office with two doors, both of which are usually open. One door opens into the hallway, while another leads into the office space for the school's administrative staff. Close by is a long desk where teachers often sit and work between classes. The availability of the table allows teachers to easily meet together and confer about students or joint projects. Students also regularly drop by and casually sit next to teachers to ask a question or seek advice.

Prominently displaying student work is, of course, something many traditional schools do, but our schools carry it to healthy extremes, because the intention goes beyond displaying pride in their students' creativity and quality work. The idea is to represent, consistently and visually, the expectations for, and possibilities of, Deeper Learning. The way in which attention is called to projects, including posters, photographs, sound speakers, circuit boards, and even model wind turbines, reinforces the substance, the application, and the methods that students are expected to engage in on a regular basis.

At High Tech High, student work—including a bicycle wheel attached to a poster explaining physics principles, and the inside of a piano with a written guide to the mechanics of music—is showcased on walls, in the labs, and even suspended from the exposed trusses on the ceiling. The practice sends clear signals that the students' work has value and is complex and that they have a standing audience of teachers, administrators, and fellow students who expect them to achieve.

Our schools also make enthusiastic use of motivational messages that convey and reinforce the schools' values. In the central lobby of Impact Academy, a display titled "Where Do Our Seniors Go?" lists the destinations of graduating seniors. Posters designed by each graduating student include photographs and descriptions of the student's career ambitions, representing future aerospace engineers, graphic designers, nurses, and psychologists. A second set of posters, completed once the students know they've been admitted to college, names the college each senior plans to attend and includes whether that student is the first- or second-generation college student in his or her family. At the end of the hallway, yet another display features the seniors' acceptance letters and admission certificates. As students report to their classes each day, they can't avoid these reminders that Impact Academy is preparing their peers, and them, for college and challenging careers. The displays are intended not to brag but to propose, encourage, and normalize an intellectual culture. In schools that have persistently struggled to develop a successful college-going culture, this sort of symbolism can be a particularly powerful tool for strengthening both hope and standards.

At Casco Bay High School, student-designed posters ti-tled "Pathways to Success" are placed throughout the build-ing and display the community's values, with mottos such as "Solve Today's Problems," "Work Independently and Collaboratively," "Investigate Deeply," and "Think Critically and Creatively."

Similarly, at Impact Academy, community goals are ex-pressed on ubiquitous posters, spelling out the school's four values: "We are Respectful; We are Safe; We Work Hard; We Support One Another." The walls also boast the core com-petencies nurtured—inquiry, analysis, research, and creative expression—and important leadership skills, such as the abil-ity to think critically, collaborate productively, communicate powerfully, and manage projects effectively. Teachers refer to the posters routinely when describing how students will be graded, and students periodically write essays about their progress in reaching them.

DEMOCRACY, AUTONOMY, AND FLEXIBILITY

Thoughtfully managing the physical environment not only has the ability to communicate high expectations, but it can also underline a school's operating style. Our schools proved to be exceptionally democratic, or at least nonhierarchical. It's rare to see teachers isolated in their rooms or gossiping in fac-ulty lounges; instead, SLA and many of the other schools pro-vide open areas with long tables where teachers meet between classes, and where students feel free to approach them. And at Avalon and the other schools, students' desks are rarely lined up in rows, but are more often arranged in circles, so that the youth end up looking at each other rather than at the back of each other's heads. No one can hide in the back row, and implicit in the setup is the idea that everyone in the room is of equal value and importance.

One of the most significant ways that Deeper Learning communities differ from the norm is that teachers enjoy an unusual degree of autonomy, at times to an extent that might seem unheard of to many teachers throughout the nation. High Tech High principal Larry Rosenstock jokingly refers to himself as "support staff," while the teacher-run Avalon School doesn't even have a principal. There, teachers commonly take on duties many traditional principals handle themselves, such as hiring staff, creating school schedules, developing partnerships with off-campus corporations and museums, and even dealing with funders. Furthermore, unlike at most traditional schools, these teachers direct their own professional development, identifying issues of common concern, planning workshops, and helping each other adapt to new technology. While this approach naturally requires highly skilled, competent professionals, it also requires a tremendous amount of trust and a willingness to truly empower educators. The roles that teachers fill in Deeper Learning will be explored more in the chapters to come.

The benefits of a school environment saturated in trust are many. Not least of them is the ability to develop a student culture that entrusts young people with as much responsibility for their education as the adults in the school. This frequently starts with the most basic and mundane features of a school, including the fact that most of them we observed don't ring bells between classes—an obvious signal that students can and should be responsible for their own schedules.

King Middle School takes this idea even further, with open-ended days that emulate real-world workplaces. David Grant, a technology integrator and teacher-training coordinator at the school, told an interviewer:

> Most schools are divided into forty- or fifty- or sixty-minute blocks. They might think they're progressive if they do eighty-minute blocks, but that's not what we're talking about. We're talking about a schedule . . . where a team of five or six experts in learning, your teachers, can say, "In order to pull off this particular project at this particular stage, in order to make the workflow happen that we need to accomplish with kids, we need to design a whole new schedule this week." And that's what we have here. . . . Nobody actually knows where anybody is most of the time, but that's the way real work happens, and we all know that. If we're working in the world and we're in any kind of engineering or design process or we're editing movies or making sounds or we're doing whatever it is that people do, nobody stops after forty minutes, puts everything down and goes on to do something else.[16]

The interplay of student and teacher autonomy is key to building safe, trusting communities and also to creating the kind of open culture necessary for meaningful learning to take place.

In this same vein, having students, rather than staff, talk to visitors and take them on campus tours was a common occurrence. The ninth graders at MC^2 STEM High School proclaimed how they have to prepare an "elevator speech" about the school to deliver to visitors. It's the small, and not so small, choices like this that let students know this is their community to shape, contribute to, and lead. And the practice of telling others about their community further ingrains in students a sense of belonging to something that values their participation.

Students are also frequently involved in other vital tasks for their schools. At Science Leadership Academy, up to forty students at a time make up the "tech squad," which is specially trained to work with the school's technology coordinator to provide support for SLA's web portal. The team also helps keep track of and maintain the schools' laptops, recording problems and even orders new parts.

At High Tech High, students are offered a deal famously pioneered at Google, whereby they can use 20 percent of their time however they choose, as long as it benefits the school—emphasizing both independent learning and the importance of the greater good. Students have stepped up to this challenge with projects including a fund-raising campaign to build a darkroom for the photography program and the invention of an app that gives visitors a smartphone guided tour of the school.

While a great many schools, including all those we visited, have student-government organizations to communicate formally with administrators, the Avalon School has a system that offers a remarkable opportunity for students to explore the nuances and complexities of governing structures. There's a constitution based on checks and balances, with an executive branch made up of teachers and a legislature representing the students. Just as in the U.S. Congress, the students can propose new laws, which must then be approved or vetoed (with an obligatory written explanation) by the executive branch.

Avalon students used their legislative power a few years ago to persuade the administration to reinstate a treasured privilege—the freedom to have lunch off campus. The staff had summarily ended the school's open lunch policy after several reports of bad behavior off campus during the forty-minute lunch period. But when the students responded with a thoughtful proposal, including a promise to end the off-campus infractions, the teachers relented, making the students feel more trusted and responsible.

Power-sharing systems like this example require both teachers and students to be creative and accountable. As a teacher at Impact Academy told us: "I believe that students can be transformed by our school, because I have been transformed by it as a teacher."

BETTER TOGETHER

Some examples we relate, such as the Casco Bay quests, are truly extraordinary in the realm of public schools. And although similar programs are certainly possible with resources and priorities directed toward Deeper Learning, our purpose in showcasing them is not for the rest of American classrooms to duplicate them as much as it is to extract and adopt the fundamental goals and principles behind the activities. It should be clear by now that building cohesive school communities, to whatever extent schools can do that, is less a luxury than a fundamental requirement for quality education.

This foundation supports the crucial goals of critical thinking, problem solving, effective communication, and learning how to learn. But in particular, it's quite easy to see how strong communities help create good collaborators. Modern education experts usually cite two reasons that collaboration has become such a key twenty-first-century skill. As employers have recognized how pooling talents can lead to more innovation and better products, collaborative efforts in the workplace are increasing. Collaboration has also become easier, and more prevalent, as new information technologies have emerged.

Many American schools by now appreciate the importance of teaching students to collaborate, and they are trying to do so by increasing the number of team projects. Unfortunately, such efforts often fail. High achievers (and their parents) may resent their being grouped with kids perceived to be low achievers, who might threaten to lower their GPAs; some projects end up being busywork, and some underprepared teachers micromanage the groups, or fail to manage them at all.

Helping students learn to work together effectively takes efforts at several levels, from inspiring students to care about each others' success, to motivating would-be idlers, to establishing procedures for constructive feedback, to knowing when and how best to intervene when group dynamics turn sour. In our travels, we found many educators who were skillful in all of these domains.

Again and again we saw teachers model collaboration for their students every day, as they worked together to design curriculum, exchange ideas about daily practices, and keep track of individual projects. They also regularly talked to their students about the value of getting along well with others by tolerating differences and taking turns.

At Impact Academy, art teacher Tyler Fister told us how he encourages students to help each other improve their work by exchanging thoughtful feedback. "They use each other as teachers," he told us. Fister gets students accustomed to the give-and-take of successful collaboration by providing an initial list of questions for them to use in their small-group discussion sessions. As they get more comfortable with the process, they gradually depend less on their teachers and more on each other.

We spoke to several teachers who told us how they take extraordinary care with their ninth- and tenth-grade students to assign them to groups that have a good chance of succeeding—making sure that there's a balance between different levels of skill, interest, and motivation. In most cases, they'll work to include in each group a leader, a motivator, an organizer, and a student who may benefit from some leading, motivating, and organizing. By the upper grades, students understand how to do this for themselves, and teachers give them more freedom to choose groups on their own.

"I know I'm a spark plug," one Rochester upperclassman told us. "I get things done, but I make sure I have an organizer to keep track of when things need to be turned in."

Teachers are constantly present as the groups do their work. While they'll step in when needed to mediate, supervise, and remind students of their deadlines, they stay on the sidelines as much as possible. At Rochester High, we watched one group working on a PowerPoint presentation of an adventure story based on historical events they were studying. Each member of the group had signed a contract specifying his or her responsibilities, and each had committed to contributing six slides to the presentation. On that day, however, one of the students was absent and hadn't turned in his slides. His flustered group leader complained to her teacher, Dan McCarthy, that she didn't know what to do. McCarthy pondered aloud: "I wonder if you have to fire him"—an option in the contract. "No!" the girl said, seeming shocked. "He's a hard worker. He should be in the group." The two of them then considered other strategies for saving the presentation.

All of the schools we profile in this book expect students to work together, in pairs or groups, much more often than what we generally see in the great majority of schools today. In most cases, as we'll elaborate in the next chapter, projects are the norm rather than the exception for schoolwork. Thus, a key part of the acculturation process for new students is for them to get used to what for many is the unfamiliar and initially uncomfortable experience of cooperating consistently with their peers.

At a dis-orientation ritual at MC^2 High School in Cleveland, we witnessed a particularly vivid example of how innovative schools help new students to both appreciate the value of collaboration and practice it with increasing skill. It came on an afternoon in which eleventh graders were leading an exercise that involved teams of freshmen competing to build the most effective penny launcher. The student leaders assigned the younger students a hypothetical budget to buy eight common items from a store, including cardboard, paper clips, pencils, soda bottles, and rubber bands. They then supervised as the teams built their launchers and subsequently tested them to see which one could throw a penny the farthest. By the end of the competition, the freshmen had not only learned about designs and prototypes, but had practiced problem solving, critical thinking, and communicating—and, perhaps most importantly, learned how to contribute to each other's success.

A BLUEPRINT FOR DEEPER LEARNING

- The development of strong school communities is essential for students to evolve from playing a passive role in their education to being active, self-directed learners.

- The most effective communities blend support and trust with high expectations and a collective responsibility for learning.

- Useful tactics to build strong learning communities include "dis-orientation" rituals to disrupt past experience; physical environments that reflect a focus on learning, openness, and equality; regular, formal, and conspicuous reminders of the community's aspirations, expectations, and norms; and the involvement of older students as mentors, models, and guides.

- Collaborating well is an increasingly necessary skill in our modern world. Teaching it is no simple exercise and requires a range of efforts, including inspiring students to care about each other's success, establishing norms for constructive feedback, stimulating those who seem less motivated, and knowing when and how to intervene—and when and how to step aside and allow students to find their way.

2

EMPOWER

ACTIVATE STUDENTS TO LEAD THEIR OWN LEARNING

"It's not give and get, but go and get."—A student at
Avalon Charter School

"THIS IS HOW KIDS WANT TO LEARN"

At King Middle School in Portland, Maine, through the Creating Currents unit, eighth graders get to see what it's like to work as a professional energy auditor, a research scientist, an energy developer, and an engineer. As auditors, armed with safety goggles, infrared thermometers, and window-draft detectors, they measure various aspects of their home energy use and write up their findings and recommendations in an industry-standard report. As scientists, studying the mechanics of wind turbines, they produce and test hypotheses to determine which variables—such as different blade sizes and shapes—contribute most effectively to wind propulsion. As developers, they write up a land-use proposal for a wind turbine that could generate electricity for the state of Maine. And as engineers, they work in teams to design and build small wind turbines, capable of generating one volt of electricity, enough to power a small LED light bulb. At the end of the project, they also take a turn as communicators, showing off their turbines at a "trade show" attended by parents and local aficionados.

The four-month, multidisciplinary unit gives kids a visceral appreciation of the nature of electricity, America's energy challenges, and the ways that each of them might eventually contribute to solutions. The teachers believe that the more actively engaged their kids are, the more easily they understand and retain the material. And these students are rarely sitting back in their chairs.

"They're up and moving nearly 90 percent of the time, investigating and designing and building things," says technology education teacher Gus Goodwin.

Many of Goodwin's students look nervous as they start these sorts of challenges. During a separate unit, the team project begins with building small robots. "First of all, I can't build anything, and I have never handled a screwdriver in my entire life," eighth grader Emma Schwartz told a TV reporter. "Like, this isn't going to work."[1] Under Goodwin's guidance, however, Schwartz and her peers were soon immersed in their work, surprising themselves—and enjoying themselves.

"This is how kids want to learn," Education Secretary Arne Duncan said, when he visited King Middle School in 2010.[2] Goodwin, a former Air Force avionics technician, was inspired to become a teacher by his fond memories of high school shop class, where he once built a pump-powered lamp. In the years since then, energy has become a much more complicated and controversial subject, but the students working on the Creating Currents project quickly find their footing. By the end of four

months, the groups were proudly showing off their wind turbines at the student trade show.

LEARNING BY DOING

"I hear and I forget," said Confucius, circa 500 B.C. "I see and I remember. I *do* and I understand." Through the centuries since then, leading educators from John Dewey onwards repeatedly have reminded us of the importance of "doing,"[3] by fully engaging and involving students in meaningful learning experiences. Providing opportunities for students to stay stimulated and active in their education is one of several tools teachers have to make their studies rich and more significant.

Larry Rosenstock, the founding principal at High Tech High, often asks his many interviewers and audiences at public talks to list the components of their most memorable high school experience. Unfailingly, he says, they'll say it was a project that involved both collaborative work and a mentor, included a fear of failure and recognition of success, and concluded with some sort of public display of the work.[4] Schools focused on Deeper Learning seek to include most, if not all, of these building blocks of meaning in their students' daily lives.[5]

Designing relevant and engaging experiences for students is a tall order, as teachers work to align projects and assignments with evolving state academic standards and also use and develop appropriate methods to ensure student work is fairly assessed. Yet on our school visits, we repeatedly were impressed by the skill with which so many teachers managed to combine authenticity and meaning with required academic content. At High Tech High in San Diego, students were helping a conservation agency find evidence against poachers in Africa by analyzing the DNA of meat sold in markets. At MC^2 STEM High School in Cleveland, they were writing original music with software and building speaker systems. At Impact Academy in Hayward, California, they were exchanging impressions about the depiction of an adolescent's experiences in a Socratic seminar focused on the popular novel *The Absolutely True Diary of a Part-Time Indian*.

As we'll elaborate, all of these experiences helped students move toward Deeper Learning. Projects that enabled students to apply what they had learned to other situations honed their problem-solving ability. Debates and Socratic seminars on issues relevant to students' daily lives bolstered their critical thinking. Required presentations made them better communicators. Teamwork strengthened their collaborative skills. And as their teachers gave them more and more responsibility, the students repeatedly rose to the challenge of becoming self-directed, expert learners.

THE OPPOSITE OF TEDIUM

The active, student-centered nature of teaching at the eight schools we visited is a powerful antidote to two longtime scourges of the education system: boredom and a passive attitude toward learning. While these problems are not new, teachers today arguably compete more than ever for scarce supplies of attention, seeking to create classroom experiences that grab students' interest and keep them engaged, while also meeting state curriculum requirements and maintaining the space to carry out fair assessments. All of that is a lot to juggle, yet we were struck by the passion for learning that we witnessed during our journeys through the schools.

Many of those we interviewed readily told us of their own painful memories of being bored in school. Says Science Leadership Academy principal Chris Lehmann:

> High school stinks, because we have to do what we're told over and over and over again. . . . I challenge all of you to go to a high school and try to sit next to a student for the entire day as you go from your 42-minute class to your 42-minute class to your 42-minute class to your 31-minute lunch, where you shove down the industrial food, to your next 42-minute class. And at the end of the day, I'll ask you not even to remember the content of your 42-minute class—just remember what *subject* it was! If you can do that, it's great. And here's the other thing, what you're told to do over and over and over again, you have no idea why or how you're ever going to need it.[6]

Although boredom has long been perceived as a character flaw, scientists have found that it is rooted in a more generalized state of anxiety,[7] and is a particularly undesirable problem for a school—ideally an environment that stimulates everyone to be alert, attentive, and engaged. While it can manifest as personal discomfort, very often boredom is correlated with negative student behavior of the sort that has contributed to the harsh disciplinary procedures being adopted in many schools throughout America. Boredom, and the often ineffective or even harmful responses to it, is also a major reason why students drop out of high school. Nearly half of 470 high school dropouts surveyed said they left school because their classes were boring and not relevant to their lives or career aspirations, as reported in a 2006 study. Add to that the half of all recent graduates who say high school is too easy and the nearly 30 percent who say they did not receive an education that prepared them for future success.[8]

The great majority of these students are from minority and low-income families, meaning the implications involved are critical to our understanding of, and ability to address, deeply rooted issues of economic and racial equity in our education system. In some metropolitan areas, urban high school graduation rates hover around 50 percent or even lower. Researchers at Johns Hopkins University identified almost two thousand high schools (about 13 percent of American high schools) where the typical freshman class shrinks by 40 percent or more by the time the students reach their senior year. These schools—schools that some have dubbed "dropout factories"—have fewer resources and more inadequately prepared teachers than schools in more affluent neighborhoods with larger numbers of white students. In fact, 38 percent of all African American students and 33 percent of all Latino students attend so-called dropout factories.[9]

These numbers highlight troubling disparities, and the news doesn't get much better when we zoom out the lens to take a collective look at all students, meaning kids from varied racial backgrounds, attending schools in cities, suburbs, and small towns. At all American high schools, fewer than one-third of all high school students are deemed ready for college. Although most aspire to get a college degree, the majority are not academically ready to do so. In fact, only 26 percent of test-takers met all of the ACT (American College Testing) college-readiness benchmarks in English, reading, math, and science. And zooming in once again, only 13 percent of all Latino secondary students met all four standards, and of African American students, only 5 percent met all four benchmarks.[10]

Frequently dismissed as a minor issue, such dire consequences make it hard to deny that the matter of disengaged students is anything but; close to 30 percent of students indicate they are bored due to lack of interaction with teachers, and 75 percent report the material being taught is not interesting.[11] Enter the aims connected to Deeper Learning. While the purpose of Deeper Learning extends well beyond just being an antidote to boredom, embracing this fuller, more engaged approach to learning is possibly one of the most effective and productive ways to avoid this major barrier to students succeeding in school and in life.

The failure of traditional schooling to adequately engage students makes it all the more significant that we found teachers managing to capture their students' attention and making sure that classroom time was purposeful, relevant, and active. What we witnessed happening with students was dramatically different from simply earning good grades or making the honor roll. Students spent considerable time "doing," whether they were working on diverse, hands-on projects, giving presentations on what they had learned, participating in seminars, or leading their own parent-teacher conferences. Teachers rarely, if ever, assumed the conventional role of the "sage on the stage." Instead, as they told us, they saw themselves as learning strategists and coaches, enabling their students to discover their own passion for learning and the best ways to go about it.

"My job is to fade into the background in a classroom," one teacher told us. "If I have planned well, the setup is good, and the directions are clear on some independent or group activity, the students can do it." While this might give the impression of a teacher doing less actual *work*, that's far from the case. This major shift in the teacher's role indeed requires fewer hours actively managing and lecturing students, but also many more in thoughtful preparation, collaborating with colleagues, and troubleshooting with students along the way.

While this kind of learning has historical roots in the theories of such philosophers and educators as John Dewey and Paulo Freire, it is also grounded in more recent research on teaching. A five-year study by researcher Fred M. Newmann and his colleagues showed that when students construct and organize knowledge, can apply disciplinary processes (scientific inquiry, historical research, literary analysis, writing) central to the subject, and communicate effectively to audiences beyond the classroom, their performance improves. Equally as important, this kind of learning is characterized by "high-level cognitive performance (i.e., rigorous, in-depth understanding instead of only a superficial acquaintance with memorized bits of knowledge) and results in personally useful products, services or productive intellectual conversations, instead of completed exercises that were contrived only for the purpose of showing competence or to please teachers."[12] Furthermore, students are most likely to be involved in what they're learning and persist at difficult tasks when they are focused on learning something or improving a skill that they care about.[13]

THE POWER—AND RIGOR—OF PROJECTS

Bear with us now for just a brief detour to explain some terminology that's probably already somewhat familiar to the teachers and principals among our readers. All of the schools we profile in this book are committed to inquiry-based learning, a teaching method developed in the 1960s as a response to traditional forms of instruction that relied on memorizing preordained content. Inquiry-based learning involves getting kids to see the big picture, question assumptions, and make connections for themselves, fueling their curiosity and contributing to their problem-solving skills.[14] For many teachers and principals committed to Deeper Learning principles, it also means encouraging kids, whenever possible, to pursue the learning paths most important to them.

Recalling his own most meaningful high school experiences, Science Leadership Academy principal Chris Lehmann said: "I remember getting deeply involved in the school TV station, where I did everything from announcing to behind-the-camera stuff. That was amazing, real, wonderful. But there were other times when I had learned how to put my head in my hand and make my pen wiggle to look like I was taking notes. It was all haphazard. But it shouldn't have to be that way."

There are several ways to make learning both real and meaningful, the focus of both this chapter and the next. One indispensable method is known as project-based learning, which falls under the umbrella of inquiry-based learning. It is an increasingly popular approach in U.S. high schools today, although it isn't always pursued in an optimal manner. The strategy has become controversial, with some critics arguing it lacks sufficient "rigor," after years in which projects were chosen haphazardly and monitored carelessly. Research suggests, however, that when implemented correctly, project-based learning is superior in many ways to conventional teaching[15]—even when it is evaluated through the lens of students' scores on academic tests. (Knowledge in Action, a multi-year study of students in three states, has shown that Advanced Placement pass rates increased by as much as 30 percent during the 2011–2012 school year when students engaged in a project-based curriculum rather than more traditional instruction.[16])

Several studies have demonstrated that effectively chosen and managed student projects can make content more memorable, improving students' problem-solving and collaborative skills, as well as their motivation.[17] In particular, this strategy has helped improve students' understanding of science and technology, in part by making learning more engaging.[18]

Not all of the teachers we observed on our school visits described what they were doing as project-based learning. Yet in all cases, we saw kids working independently or in groups on projects that *they* conceptualized and executed. At all the schools, too, we found teachers helping students sharpen their critical-thinking skills by following a general strategy aptly described by Stanford's Linda Darling-Hammond, who explains the trick is to "problematize" subject matter by having students "define problems and treat claims and explanatory accounts, even those offered by 'experts' as needing evidence."[19]

For schools that have long held to traditional teaching methods, switching to more project-based learning won't be easy. Yet as states move forward with the Common Core State Standards, it will increasingly be necessary. Smarter Balanced, one of the assessment organizations, recently released a sample assessment task asking high school juniors to "engage strategically in collaborative and independent inquiry to investigate/research topics, pose questions, and gather and present information."

For now, however, many teachers we spoke to said they still face critics who worry that education can't be rigorous if students aren't quietly sitting at desks. "There's a false dichotomy between meaningful exploration and rigor," says Casco Bay High School English teacher Susan McCray. "In fact, you cannot have true rigor without meaning. It's nice to think that your textbooks and tests are rigorous, but if no one is reading them because his or her head is on the desk, then you have no learning (and no rigor). When students know they are doing real work that matters, they are committed and push themselves towards true excellence." Other teachers we interviewed told similar stories, contending they weren't sacrificing any state-required content in exchange for providing their students with powerful, real-life experiences.

"If you are going to jump out of a plane, who do you want to pack your parachute?" says Gus Goodwin, at King Middle School, elaborating: "Someone who did well on a test on parachute packing or someone who learned firsthand how to do it from a professional, then tried it, made some mistakes, and learned from her mistakes and then packed it perfectly and can explain how and why she packed it that way?" Most (though certainly not all) educators would agree with us that thoughtful, meaningful testing and assessments are a valuable tool for educators. But they are just that—a tool, a means to better support student learning—and should never be mistaken for the end.

STAND AND DELIVER

At Rochester High School in Indiana, science teacher Amy Blackburn assigned a group of seven senior students to design a more efficient emergency room for the local hospital. Blackburn was uniquely qualified to orchestrate this project, having worked in a hospital lab for seven years before she became a teacher. Yet here it's time for a quick caveat, which is that by using her story, and that of Gus Goodwin, a former avionics instructor, we by no means intend to imply that teachers have to bring this particular sort of specialized knowledge into their classrooms. In fact, almost all teachers—just like their students—have unique gifts, interests, and specialized knowledge that should be tapped and utilized in their teaching for the benefit of student learning. The stories we've chosen to illustrate Deeper Learning are meant to be understood as examples, not formulas. And as you'll see later on in this chapter, teachers with all kinds of backgrounds—even traditional ones—use them successfully.

The job Blackburn assigned involved several challenging tasks. The students began by doing research to understand factors that increase or limit hospital efficiency. They downloaded scholarly articles on emergency room procedures including staffing, the tracking of patients, and typical wait times. Next, they identified key issues and developed a set of questions for further investigation, after which they toured the existing emergency room, interviewing doctors and nurses. Finally, the group came up with two innovations to improve the ER's efficiency, and wrote up formal proposals describing how their plans might be implemented. Specifically, they suggested that the ER have two separate waiting rooms, to triage for patients needing more immediate care, and that there be an appointment system for patients who didn't need to be seen right away.

All of this, of course, was already more intellectually demanding than many a high school student's daily fare. But Blackburn expected more. Early on in the project, she informed her students that she had arranged for them to present their recommendations to a couple of ER nurses and school administrative staff.

Blackburn's students weren't slouchers. Yet from the moment they began anticipating having to present their work, they worked harder. With the date set for the public presentation, they scrambled to organize their thoughts and refine their PowerPoint files. On the night of the presentation, in one of the high school classrooms, the audience members asked pointed questions—and the students were prepared.

As anyone who has ever given a public speech knows, preparing such a talk focuses the mind. We continually noted how teachers at our eight schools recognized the power of public-speaking events to motivate students to do quality work, and they often require some kind of public presentation in addition to having students simply hand in their assignments.

At King Middle School, the students who complete the Creating Currents unit display their model turbines, land reports, and energy audits at a booth alongside professional and environmental groups in an annual Green Expo held on the school's campus. The students explain their work to passersby, and at the end of the event compete for an award that goes to the turbine designer who displays the greatest "creativity, outrageousness, ingenuity, or inspiration."

Similarly, for a unit that focused on the arts, freshmen at MC^2 in Cleveland presented their projects, including poems, plays, music, and stereo speakers they designed and built themselves, at an annual event at the Rock and Roll Hall of Fame. Pride is a great motivator, and we saw countless teachers skilled at cultivating it in the service of learning. Besides preparing formal presentations, students also frequently engage in public debates, which obliges them to engage in research material, consider multiple perspectives, demonstrate their mastery in the subject at hand, and, of course, improve their communication skills.

At High Tech High, former world history teacher Dan Wise is such a strong believer in debates that he has organized every course he teaches as leading up to thirty-five-minute debates on six historical topics that are central to each course. Before he throws students into this demanding routine, Wise takes great care to prepare them. Over the years, he has designed a set of activities to help kids develop the many skills required in debate, from conducting research to writing a two-page "historical brief" on their topic to help them prepare. In addition to serving as a reference tool for the debate, the brief helps develop students' writing and organization skills, including the capacity to summarize and cite multiple sources, and use graphs and timelines to represent information.

To further help students prepare for debates, Wise assigns them to small groups to review each others' briefs and offer feedback, while he walks from group to group to help them identify questions that will make their arguments stronger. As one class prepared to debate on the U.S. role in Syria, for instance, Wise suggested they consider questions such as: What form of government does Syria have? What is the United States' historical relationship with Syria and its government? What is the relationship between Syria and Israel? Why does that matter to the United States?

Wise makes sure each group comes up with two additional questions of their own, as well as ten to fifteen researched facts relating to their topic. He keeps track of students' progress with periodic check-ins, encouraging kids who seem to be struggling to practice their arguments with him. The process is as collaborative as it is competitive: students prepare to argue on either side of the debate, and won't know which side they'll be taking until shortly before show time. "I don't want students to see the debates as a zero-sum game," Wise says. Similarly, after the debate is over and student observers hand in a verdict, Wise never tells the debaters who won or lost.

CRITICAL THINKERS

One reason these teachers rely so heavily on formal presentations and debates is that they understand how the social nature of learning contributes to the development of robust critical-thinking skills. Strong relationships and enthusiastic conversations, not only between teachers and students, but between the students themselves, keenly motivate students to do their best. Another tool of this approach is the Socratic seminar—a "teacherless class" in which students discuss a text or idea they are studying, using open-ended questions. As with debates, seminar participants must learn how to express their views, back up their arguments with evidence, and listen carefully and respectfully to their peers. Several of our schools rely on these seminars to sharpen communication and critical-thinking skills, two major Deeper Learning objectives.

At the Impact Academy in California, English teacher Hannah Odyniec spends four to six weeks preparing her freshmen students to participate in the seminars during school-wide exhibitions to which families are invited. If the ninth graders seem extraordinarily poised and confident on stage, it is due to the hours of repeated practice, with progressive exercises in expressing their positions, supporting their claims, and listening to each other respectfully, until these skills start to become second nature.

On our visit to the school, we watched a group of about nine students pull their desks into a circle as they prepared to discuss the 2007 young-adult novel *The Absolutely True Diary of a Part-Time Indian*, by Sherman Alexie. A second group of equal size, which was taking a turn as observers, arranged their chairs in a concentric circle on the outskirts of the first, and silently began taking notes.

The seminar began with one of the students asking why the protagonist's friends treat him like a traitor for transferring to an affluent high school outside the reservation.

"Were they really his friends?" the student asked.

"That's a good point," responded another, who had obviously registered his teacher's injunctions to listen respectfully. "Was he really ever accepted where he was? Wasn't it better to start over, even if the kids in the school were white and rich?"

By the time we saw them in action, the students had practiced several standard phrases that helped them let each other know they were listening closely to each other's contributions. "That's a good point," was just one tool they had to show agreement and support, others being, "That is an interesting idea," "I had not thought of that before," and "I see what you mean."

Their repertoire also included ways to paraphrase what they had just heard, to make sure they fully understood—such as, "So you are saying that . . ." or "In other words, you think that . . ." or "What I hear you saying is . . ."—as well as ways to politely seek clarification, with phrases such as, "I have a question about that." In cases of disagreement, students had been trained to justify their positions, with openings such as, "I got a different answer than you because . . ." or "I see it a different way because. . . ."

As the students in the inner circle carried on their discussion, the observers in the outer circle listened intently. Each of them had been assigned specific tasks, which among other objectives would help their teacher assess each participant's performance. Some of the observers had been asked to record at least five main points made in the discussion. Others were looking for five positive contributions made by inner-circle participants, with the instruction to list those who supported their opinions with evidence from the text, those who asked thoughtful questions that moved the conversation forward, those who listened respectfully to peers and built off of comments made by others, and those who made insightful comments and connections. One student was counting the number of comments, questions, and references to the text made by each student, while another was writing down comments on the overall dynamics of the seminar, and yet another was noting at least five comments that she would have made had she been a participant.

Just like the inner-circle members, the observers had been well coached on procedure, and used similarly standard phrases as they kept their notes. For instance, they gave "props" (shorthand for "proper respect"), as in "Props to Tanya for starting off the conversation and giving reference to the text" or "Props to Annette for putting your hand up but then taking it down because you realized you may have been talking too much."

Odyniec, holding a stopwatch in one hand and pen in the other as she jotted down notes, spoke only a few times during the seminar. She stepped in to help only when students were clearly struggling, and occasionally offered remarks that modeled skillful participation, gently pressing the seminar members to back up their statements with evidence. "Where do you see that in the text?" she asked at one point, and "Is that what the passage really means?"

"Students are so anxious to get their ideas out there that they often just argue," she later explained to us. "We need to develop their habits to be about articulating where you found the evidence and to back up every argument with evidence. Then our job is to help them practice that daily." Odyniec said she knows the class has been a success when she hears students continue the discussion as they leave her classroom. And, in fact, she added, "It's rare that they don't."

"SCHOOL IS REVISION"

For students to become deeper learners, they need to get used to the idea that learning is never a finite process, and that it certainly shouldn't end as soon as they hand in a quiz or an essay. In all the schools we visited, students get frequent opportunities to revise their work many times, in response to feedback from teachers and peers. In this way, they come to understand just how much effort is required to produce high-quality work.

"School is revision," David Grant, the technology integrator at King Middle School, told us. In other words, the point of schoolwork is learning and understanding, not checking tasks off lists. This means that assessment of a student never ends with the student's failure, Grant said. The first iteration of a project or draft of a paper is always just that—a starting point in a "learning loop" of work, feedback, reflection, and revision.

Revision is particularly important at schools such as MC^2 that use mastery-based learning. Under that system, students won't pass a class if they don't achieve a rating of Mastery or Exceeds Mastery (the two other possible ratings are Incomplete and No Work). The students know they will be expected to keep working on projects until they get them right.

Revision is a hallowed regimen at most schools committed to Deeper Learning goals. Both teachers and students understand that schedules must allow plenty of time for it, with students often spending time in class refining their assignments. Teachers work one-on-one with students during class and after school, while also coordinating peer feedback and revisions undertaken by student teams. At Rochester High, one teacher always tells his class that they need to understand that "without three drafts, your product won't be that good."

At King Middle School, students are given a handout to

follow that assesses the scientific content, data analysis, and writing quality of the home energy audit they conduct in their Creating Currents unit. They refer to it first as they edit their own work and then as a tool for peer review as they share drafts in pairs and small groups. Only then will teachers step in to offer their own feedback.

King science teacher Peter Hill says he and his colleagues will coach students to interpret data carefully, and "decide what the numbers mean before they begin writing. We sometimes break their writing down sentence by sentence. This is what I found; this is what it means. We work through it again and again." This process, while laborious, helps students build their character as well as their academic portfolio. They have opportunities to become more patient, reflective, responsive, perseverant, and resilient, as well as ambitious to improve the quality of their work. We heard from many kids who understood and valued these opportunities to grow. "Before, I was a minimalist in school," one Casco Bay senior told us. "I did just enough to get my passing grade and quit. But here, it makes you want to do your best the first time, and if it isn't enough, the revision system helps you improve."

Before there can be any useful revision, of course, there must be reflection. Teachers at our eight schools say they constantly coach students in this skill, talking about the value of reflection all the time, and regularly assigning them to make entries in journals or on blogs. One social studies teacher at the Avalon School has her students write a blog reflection on every project, while a teacher at King Middle School has students write in their journals every week. King math students typically write in journals to explain how they arrived at answers to specific problems.

"Reflection is a big part of everything we do," says Casco Bay High School biology teacher Ben Donaldson. "It's a running joke that the students are professional reflectors."

STUDENTS TAKE THE LEAD

A particularly vivid example of putting students in the driver's seat of their own education is the way they handle what traditional schools refer to as parent-teacher conferences. At these time-honored encounters, it's not uncommon for students to stay home while the adults discuss their progress or lack thereof. But at schools built on Deeper Learning principles, the meetings are often turned into *student-led* conferences, with students presenting their schoolwork, while their teachers, having helped them prepare, sit across the table, or even off to the side. The triad then sits together to review and discuss the work and the student's progress. The message, once again, is that the students are responsible for their own success.

The specific dynamics of these conferences vary widely. At California's Impact Academy, three or four different sets of students and their families meet simultaneously, as teachers circulate through the room, making sure parents are getting their questions answered, and only intervening if the student is struggling. Yet in all cases, the basic spirit is the same: this is the student's moment to share his or her reflections on achievements and challenges.

At King Middle School, the twice-yearly student-led conferences are "one of the most important things we do to have students own their own learning," says Peter Hill, who helps prepare kids in his advisory class, or crew, for their meetings. "And yet, the students' first impulse is to tear through their folders to find every best thing that they have done to show their parents."

Instead, Hill encourages students to reflect on the connection between the effort they have made and the quality of their work. To this end, he asks them to choose three examples that help them tell their parents a deeper story: one that shows they have recognized both a personal strength and an area in which they are struggling. Most students, he says, have never thought about their learning in this way. Nor have most of their parents.

Indeed, many parents need some time to adjust to the new format, Hill acknowledges. Often, he says, a mother or father "just wants to ask me about how their child is doing, or how they are behaving. Sometimes I have to nudge the conversation back to let the child lead. We also have to teach the parents how to be reflective about their kids' work and how best to help."

Eventually, however, most if not all parents appreciate the new process, teachers told us. "They come to realize that report cards don't tell them anything very useful," says Gus Goodwin, Hill's colleague. "And over time, the parents begin to set a higher bar for their students at these conferences."

As crew leader, Hill has his students practice how they'll discuss their work products with their parents. We watched as he spoke with one eighth-grade boy who initially shyly lowered his head as he confessed that he felt uncomfortable showing his work to anyone, including his mother and father.

Hill told the boy he understood how he felt, and then offered some strategies for discussing his work in math, which both of them knew was a problem area. "You have done some good work of which you should be proud," he told him. Together, they then picked out a paper that demonstrated the boy's effort, after which Hill suggested: "When we have the conference, why don't you use this assignment and begin by saying, 'I have done a good job in math when I . . . .'" The boy wrote the phrase in his notebook, and visibly began to relax, after which Hill used the rest of the advisory period to find more examples of work that showed his effort.

As kids learn to advocate for themselves in this way, they discover how to let their parents know more specifically how to support them. Hill tells the story of one student who was clearly intelligent, but struggling with his independent reading. Rambunctious in class, the boy surprised Hill by sitting straight and quietly in his chair when his father, a seemingly stern man, walked into the room. But what surprised him even more was when the boy spoke up for himself during the conference, telling his father: "I realize now that I need to spend more time reading on my own and I need your help with that. I need my three brothers out of the room at night so I can read in silence."

Such exchanges empower both students and their parents, Hill noted, adding: "When I checked in on the student a few weeks later, he was very pleased that his dad was keeping his brothers out of his room so he could do his silent reading."

At Science Leadership Academy, health educator Pia Martin coaches her students in how to communicate with parents about difficult topics, such as why they might have received a C in a class. "How will your parents respond?"

she asks. "What are the things that will trigger your parents and how will that play out? Will this lead to lost privileges or other forms of punishment? How do we minimize this?"

"In conference, I'm your advocate," she always reminds them. Like Hill and several other teachers we spoke with, Martin said she usually helps begin conferences by encouraging students to talk about what they are good at, to prevent meetings from turning into blame-fests. She tells the students to start the meeting with two questions: "What do I do well?" and "How can I build on this?"

"I always tell them, 'Own what you got,'" Martin says. Only after students spend a moment to recognize what they're doing right does she encourage them to tackle the challenges, with the following questions: "What have I not done well?" and "How can I improve this?"

TAKING STOCK

In a strategy similar to the student-parent conferences, teachers at the Deeper Learning schools we observed required students to make formal presentations of what they had achieved at key moments during their school careers. Again, this process helps make students more responsible and actively engaged in their learning. Just the thought of standing up in public to explain a project or essay usually inspires students to work harder to ensure it's a quality product.

At Impact Academy, students must complete and defend their schoolwork two times during their four years of high school: once at the end of the sophomore year, with a

Benchmark Portfolio, and again just before they graduate, with a College Success Portfolio.

A completed Benchmark Portfolio is composed of four pieces of student work, approved by teachers, from that student's first two years. The student must also provide a cover letter detailing the contents and reflecting on each piece of work, discussing what was learned along the way. Then, he or she selects three samples of work to defend in front of an Oral Defense Committee made up of teachers.

We observed one student's PowerPoint presentation, which started off with a picture of her as a child and a note about her ambition to understand patents and one day own her own retail clothing business. She included a slide about her achievements in school, on completing her work on time and getting good grades, and listed among her challenges "group work" and "being a leader." The remainder of her presentation focused on her three work samples: a science lab write-up, an essay analyzing the book *Night* for her English class, and a collage she had made in her art class. She wound up by telling her teachers how she planned to use what she had learned to work harder and learn more in her final two years.

Impact Academy seniors also follow an annual routine, although in this case the narrative is more directed toward the student's readiness to go on to college and a career. One of the components of the portfolio must be a project completed during the required workplace internship. Students begin thinking about their College Success Portfolios as soon as they begin junior year, since they know they have to produce a minimal number of high-quality projects that they'll be able to include. Each project must be "certified" by teachers, which always requires several rounds of feedback and revision. "We get as many of them certified as we can," one Impact student told us. "You want to have plenty to choose from. You have plenty of tries in your junior and senior year. You have to manage your time and then you can revise and revise."

At High Tech High in San Diego, students present similar portfolios at the end of each academic year in a ritual called Transitional Presentations of Learning—ten-minute speeches given by the students followed by questions and answers, which may be attended by parents, teachers, and classmates. Students maintain a digital portfolio of their work throughout the year in preparation for this event, and are responsible for updating it every semester, which encourages them to reflect and revise. Students take these presentations very seriously, practicing for hours and dressing up to go onstage.

At the Avalon School in Minnesota, seniors culminate their school career with a public presentation of a project they have worked on all year. The half-hour presentations begin in May and last for up to four weeks, with up to four students presenting every afternoon and evening. Parents, extended family members, peers, and interested professionals attend, as does a committee made up of teachers and one outside expert in the student's chosen topic.

Most of the presentations involve PowerPoint or Prezi, while some students also incorporate film, music, or dance. The student presentation is followed by an extended period of questioning, after which someone usually delivers a bouquet of flowers. The experience is often rounded out by the teens heading out to celebrate with their families.

FAIL SAFE

When students engage more actively with their work, as they do in all of our schools, they invest more of themselves in terms of energy as well as time. This not only often leads to more creativity and better mastery than does the standard fare of memorization and test-taking, but also familiarizes kids more directly with the real-world experience of occasionally painful failure. It's one thing to get a D on a term paper; it's another to watch a robot designed as a group project explode, and yet another to lose your place in a classroom presentation, or worse, in front of the whole school. The feedback is more personal, and, yes, often more painful, but the outcomes are probably healthier over the long term, teaching reflection and resilience. In other words, both the risks and rewards are greater, and more lasting.

The teachers we interviewed encourage students to keep taking the risks, conveying high expectations that the youth will rise to challenges and bounce back from setbacks. It calls to mind the popular Silicon Valley mantra "fail early and often," since for successful entrepreneurs there's no reward without risk, and no risk without occasional failure. As Harvard psychologist Howard Gardner has written, high-achieving people share a special talent for "identifying their own strengths and weaknesses, for accurately analyzing the events of their own lives, and for converting into future successes those inevitable setbacks that mark every life."[20]

The teachers we witnessed frequently urge their students to embrace setbacks as gifts, and reflect on the value of failure. As King Middle School teacher Gus Goodwin's eighth graders were building prototypes for the LEGO Robotics Challenge, he asked them to reflect, in writing, on a quote by the author and engineer Henry Petroski, an expert in failure analysis: "Success is success, but that is all that it is. It is failure that brings improvement." Goodwin asked the kids to consider a specific time during the challenge when they experienced failure, and relate how that failure led to improvement. He and others feel confident that the students will be able to learn from their failures if they can do so in a supportive environment where they know they won't be teased, and also have sufficient time to reflect.

Scientists have fairly recently established that, contrary to common opinion, resilience isn't an inborn trait, but the product of a complex system in which a child becomes strong at least in part due to other people's belief in him or her.[21] Teachers at our schools are determined to play that role, encouraging their students to give projects their all, and to learn to fail—safely.

A BLUEPRINT FOR DEEPER LEARNING

- Active and meaningful educational experiences are key in helping students reach Deeper Learning goals—and also make a difference in graduation rates, rendering engaged learning experiences a critical component of any plan or process to curb high school dropout rates.

- Schools that embrace Deeper Learning objectives take care to get students doing real-world projects, such as completing energy assessments of their homes or designing a new emergency room for a local hospital. School routines that rely on a lot of group and independent work, including project-based learning, can not only help students figure out what they're good at, but also give teachers and students opportunities not available in traditional class-rooms to learn about each other spontaneously and strengthen their relationships to each other and to learning.

- Practice makes perfect—or, at least, a lot better. Students most efficiently and successfully become deeper learners when their teachers can devote their talent and a significant amount of time to devising learning loops that provide useful feedback and op-portunities to revise work and practice new skills.

- Guiding students through revisions of their work is a fundamentally important strategy for Deeper Learning.

- Teachers can encourage students to think critically and care more about the quality and impact of their work by requiring oral presentations, ranging from debates and Socratic seminars to student-led parent conferences and public speeches.

3

CONTEXTUALIZE

TIE SUBJECTS TO EACH OTHER AND KEEP IT REAL

"Do any of us live in a compartmentalized world in a compartmentalized way? For instance, do I say, 'I am going to do the math part of my house project now. And in forty-five minutes I will do the science part of my house project'? . . . When things are so disjointed, they become discrete tasks and don't have purpose and meaning."
—**Susan McCray, English teacher at Casco Bay High School**

"When students are exposed to real experiences rather than simulated ones, they have a context for learning."—**Diana Laufenberg, American history teacher at Science Leadership Academy**

CLIMBING MT. DOCUMENTARY

At 4 a.m. on an April morning in Portland, Maine, fifty-seven Casco Bay high school students, four teachers, and five parents piled into a school bus and several vans, at the start of a sixteen-

hour drive to Franklin, a one-street town in the Appalachian mountains of West Virginia.

During their weeklong stay in rustic dorms at the Almost Heaven Habitat for Humanity site, as part of a program called the Junior Journey, the students would interview and photograph families living in or waiting for a Habitat home, with the goal of producing a multimedia documentary about Appalachian poverty. Their task would be ambitious even for adult professionals, added to which is the fact that for this group of teens, most of whom have never traveled out of state, rural West Virginia is a far cry from the familiar environs of Maine.

In their favor, however, the kids had been expertly and thoroughly prepared. They had spent much of the past two years getting ready for their trip, as had their teachers, with preparations including a five-week crash course on video journalism and Southern culture. Professional documentary producers helped teach them to use cameras and microphones and to conduct illuminating interviews. In their humanities class, they learned about bluegrass music, while also studying about coal-mining communities and how fossil fuels became important in manufacturing during the Industrial Revolution. In English, they read novels about poverty, including The Grapes of Wrath *and* Their Eyes Were Watching God. *In chemistry, they learned about the carbon cycle and how burning coal produces greenhouse gases.*

After studying the mechanics of climate change, the students had developed policy proposals, ranging from promoting tidal power to regulating fracking, which they thoroughly researched and formally presented to a panel of experts at an Environmental Symposium in downtown Portland.

Throughout this time, the students also had plenty of opportunities to reflect on what they were learning, guided by two questions central to their project: "How does a community sustain itself in the face of resource degradation and economic adversity?" and "What impact will you have as a generation?" And as additional preparation, all of them by then were used to working in teams, having collaborated to raise $40,000 for their expenses and having planned logistics for a journey that their English teacher and expedition leader, Susan McCray, compared to climbing a mountain.

"When you're in the mountains, everything is so real, and there's an urgency, a vitality, and sense of purpose that is deep and heartfelt," she told us. "At the same time, just as if we're in the mountains, we're exploring things from all angles, which is how the real world works. Everything in our world—unlike most schoolrooms—is interconnected and multifaceted. When you give kids the opportunity to explore the world that way, there's not only more positive spirit, there are opportunities for much deeper thinking."

NO LOOSE TIES

In the previous chapter, we emphasized the importance of learning experiences that are active and engaging for the students involved. In the following pages, we will delve into a particularly powerful way to add meaning to learning, which is to make the subject matter both *integrated* and *relevant*.

High school students throughout the United States commonly complain that they can't see why they have to learn much of what they're required to study, because they'll never need it in "real life." But you won't often hear this lament at schools that embrace Deeper Learning. At these innovative institutions, curricula are carefully and strategically integrated, so that what students learn in one class is meaningful and applicable in another. Additionally, teachers constantly remind students of the real-world relevance of what they're learning by explicitly building the "real" into assignments and units, and, as we'll see more directly in the next chapter, by taking students into the world and bringing the world into school, to make real life a natural part of the learning process.

Unfortunately, this approach to learning remains a rarity in traditional U.S. classrooms. The norm there is what Atlanta-based school administrator Tyler S. Thigpen calls a "subject-centered approach," in which "the emphasis is on gaining content knowledge, developing skills within disciplines, and advancing academic levels." In this view of learning, as Thigpen explains, mastering math, science, and English theoretically equips students for their futures, whereas, in fact, it does just the opposite, training them in unrealistic expectations of how the world actually works.[1]

"Do any of us live in a compartmentalized world in a compartmentalized way?" asks Casco Bay's Susan McCray. "For instance, do I say, 'I am going to do the math part of my house project now. And in forty-five minutes I will do the science part of my house project'? . . . When things are so disjointed, they become discrete tasks and don't have purpose and meaning."

The antidote is what Thigpen calls a relationship-centered strategy,[2] in which classroom objectives are frequently, explicitly related to the real world, and students focus on topics that transcend the disciplines by tackling authentic problems, such as nuclear proliferation or world hunger.

That's certainly the approach at Casco Bay High School, where Sustainability and Resource Degradation, a nine-month-long unit, includes the Appalachia Unplugged subunit and wraps the junior-year curriculum into an integrated study of impoverished rural communities and fossil fuel dependence, culminating in student productions of policy proposals, videos, and public presentations. "Everything is related," says McCray. "Everything matters, and we are all working all the time to help them see the connections. Everything is also integrated, so they can see and feel the meaning and purpose of what they are doing."

Neuroscientists have established the power of this kind of learning: memories are easier to retain when they are connected with each other and personally meaningful.[3] And just as with project-based learning, described in the previous chapter, research shows that when the strategy of integrating classes is done right, it improves students' engagement and understanding—and academic success.[4]

MISSING LINKS

Change is never easy, and we realize it would take a major transition for traditional schools to shift from their current approach of teaching subjects in isolation to the relationship-centered model we advocate. What's standing in the way, more than anything, is the manner in which most American schools are structured and run. Traditional, top-down procedures grant teachers little or no time to collaborate as teams, something that is essential for developing interrelated learning plans (among other worthy pursuits). Indeed, teachers in traditional schools often say they barely have time in the day merely to teach their classes, grade homework, and deal with the additional common demands from students, their parents, and school staff.

Linda Darling-Hammond has found that the average time allotted to U.S. teachers for planning lessons is three to five hours a week, which they're expected to use by themselves. In contrast, she says, teachers in other industrialized nations, including France, Germany, China, and Japan, on average are given from ten to twenty hours a week to work together planning lessons, observe one another in the classroom, and meet individually with parents and students.[5]

This is more akin to what we've seen in Deeper Learning schools, with some of the time built into teachers' daily schedules and the rest freed up automatically as a byproduct of the schools' common policy of having students spend much of their time working independently or in groups. These comparatively flexible teacher schedules are one of the biggest factors contributing to what we found to be an extraordinary amount of motivation—and success—among the teachers we encountered.

We found teachers routinely meeting together in groups organized by grade level or by academic classes, as they worked on collaborative and integrated projects. These meetings were in addition to occasional conferences involving the entire teaching staff to discuss major upcoming events.

At King Middle School, grade-level teachers meet every other day for seventy minutes at a time, in addition to working together every Wednesday afternoon when the students are released early. Besides this, and before each school year starts, King teachers attend a five-day "leadership summit" together, sharing ideas on learning experiences.

Similarly, at the Avalon School, teachers meet twice a week in the morning for seventy-five minutes. At High Tech High, teachers meet for an hour every day before the students arrive. At several schools we visited, teachers routinely lunch together, specifically to extend their time for collaboration. As Casco Bay, Spanish teacher Nancy Hagstrom told us: "If you think you are going to come to school, go into your classroom, shut the door, and not see or talk to another teacher the rest of the day, then this school is not for you."

These distinct features designed to provide teachers with the flexibility, time, and support to communicate with each other and students are essential components of professional learning communities (PLCs), environments that cultivate and nurture all aspects of Deeper Learning.

QUESTIONS AS GUIDES

At Impact Academy in Hayward, California, a student told us what it's like to be plunged into inquiry-based learning, nudged along by teachers who seemingly never are satisfied with simple answers. "Everything is *why* here," the student said. "You give an answer, the teacher asks why. Where did you get your information from? Why do you think this? You can't say, 'Just because.' You have to give evidence. You have to have answers. . . . You'll get a five-paragraph essay assigned, and by the end it's five pages, because they keep asking you why."

These teachers also maintain a similar practice among themselves, as they goad each other on in planning integrated units that will help students learn most meaningfully and effectively.

When teachers develop the kind of multidisciplinary plan for units such as Casco Bay's Appalachia Unplugged, for instance, they often start by asking each other's ideas about the most compelling questions related to required curriculum for that year, while keeping in mind key Deeper Learning goals. What issues will best push students to think critically? What questions will best motivate them to do significant research and learn to evaluate evidence? How can students take what they've learned in one subject and apply it to another? How can they develop their problem-solving and communication skills by building on what they've learned to devise solutions to real-world problems?

We saw how these sorts of questions—and the way teachers collaborated to keep asking them—helped build the framework for the Creating Currents unit at King Middle School, described in the preceding chapter. Subsequently, when students reported to their English class, their teacher was prepared to help them write up the results of the home energy audit they had completed in their science class. Their math teacher coached them on how to calculate their carbon footprint—the fossil fuel energy they use in their daily activities. And after they embarked on building their wind turbines in science class, their English teacher worked with them again, this time to help prepare a five-paragraph persuasive essay supporting or opposing wind power that integrated what they had learned about greenhouse gases and responses to potential community concerns about the siting of large wind farms.

Two questions link together everything the eighth graders at King study over the ten weeks of the unit: "How do we capture and use nature's energy?" and "How can you change your energy consumption to improve the world?"

"What makes this Deeper Learning is that the students are putting all of the parts together to view a wider expanse of using alternative energy," King social studies teacher Mark Gervais told us. "In social studies, they learn where the wind turbines are located and why, while in English they learn how to persuade, and not just shout."

The MC² STEM school in Cleveland uses similar strategies. Major themes, called capstones, connect different classes for three months at a time. Given that one of the freshman themes is Bridges, for instance, math students use tools from trigonometry to understand the structure and stability of bridges, while English and social studies students explore the metaphorical and historical implications of bridges as they read Shakespeare's *Romeo and Juliet* (and consider the ways in which romantic love can "bridge" or divide families) and learn about the integral role of the U.S. civil rights movement as a bridge to a more equitable society. The Bridges unit includes a field trip to visit bridges in the Cleveland area and provides students in an engineering class the opportunity to build a model bridge, using physics and engineering principles.

In tenth grade, when one of the themes is The Age of Enlightenment, students will read Plato's "The Allegory of the Cave" in English class and design and build a "light box" in their science course. Studying the literal properties of light and shadows reinforces the power of Plato's analogies about the power of logic and reason. MC²'s principal, Jeff McClellan, says the capstone concept has proven to be so effective that Egypt's Ministry of Education recently decreed that its schools would adopt it.

In Philadelphia, Science Leadership Academy likewise uses themes to build connections between courses—in this case with the twist that the themes themselves are interrelated and also comparatively broad. The freshman theme, for instance, is Identity and the Self, while for sophomores it's the Self and Systems. For juniors, it's Change in the Self and Systems, and for seniors, it's Creation. These themes offer an emotional context for material such as the evolution of the U.S. political system, which students undertake in eleventh grade. Diana Laufenberg told us that when she teaches a unit on Political Participation and Suffrage, conveying how previously excluded groups such as African Americans and women have gained the right to vote, she'll ask questions such as "How has the right to vote affected the development of the country through history?" and "What is the role of the individual in the electoral process?"

"We explore the interplay between the electoral system and the individual throughout history," Laufenberg explained, adding that she takes care to draw connections between history and students' contemporary lives. "Politicians' decisions affect the lives of individuals daily, and understanding how they can empower themselves with information to work within the system to make change is huge."

Once they've become familiar with the evolution of voting rules and the Electoral College, Laufenberg's students apply what they have learned by proposing a constitutional amendment to change one aspect of the electoral rules—such as voting age, electoral college configuration, qualifications for voting, or conditions by which a citizen may be disenfranchised—to help make the process more democratic. The students work in groups to develop language for the amendment and write position papers justifying their choices.

They also prepare strategies to pass the amendment, predicting which groups of Americans might support it, anticipating and answering potential criticism, and, finally, planning radio and TV ads in favor of their plan.

Laufenberg times her unit to end right after Election Day, so that students are motivated to pay more attention to the real-world campaigns occurring around them. She assigns her students to visit their neighborhood polling places on the day of the vote. They go out in pairs, armed with video cameras and a letter of introduction from Laufenberg (and with her cell phone number handy in case of any problems), and interview voters about their voting habits, including how informed they are about the issues on the ballot and what impact they believe their vote will have. Returning to class, they share the videos and talk about what they encountered.

As Laufenberg explained, the task of interviewing voters at the polls "takes away the mystery of voting for a group of students who are within a year or less of being able to vote themselves. Students observe democracy up close, interacting with their own neighbors in conversation about the voting system, and then reflecting on their own future as an active citizen engaged in the democratic process. When students are exposed to real experiences rather than simulated ones, they have a context for learning and can develop multiple levels of knowledge and skills."

"WHAT IF SCHOOL WERE REAL LIFE?"

It's common—for educators, parents, policymakers, and even students—to assume that schools are meant to prepare kids for real life, despite how very little like real life they usually are. In contrast, teachers and principals at Deeper Learning schools are constantly looking for ways to break down the barriers, posing the question voiced by Chris Lehmann, principal of Science Leadership Academy: "What if school *were* real life?"

The teachers we interviewed endeavor as much as possible to connect students' studies to events in the real world. Controversy isn't avoided; it's often a key part of the curricula. This not only makes classwork more stimulating, but gives students practice in critical thinking, problem solving, and effective communication, while contributing to their transformation into more informed and thoughtful citizens. At High Tech High, for instance, the humanities and math teachers developed a joint project tying the current mortgage crisis and growth of personal debt to concepts in math as well as social studies.

As with Diana Laufenberg's class at SLA, teachers we interviewed often link classwork with local, state, or national elections. At King Middle School, for example, sixth-grade teachers designed an in-depth, cross-disciplinary unit linking all of their courses at that time to the 2012 presidential election. In English class, the students designed and wrote a "palm card," the small cards candidates hand to voters, with their own short autobiographies. In math, they used sample election returns to learn basic statistical concepts. In science, they studied environmental issues that were raised in the state campaigns, while in music, students wrote song lyrics about the election.

All eighty of the sixth graders and their teachers also visited the local Republican and Democratic headquarters, where staff members talked to them about the election process and how people design campaigns. Students were able to ask questions and learn how campaign organizers use volunteers and identify likely voters. On other days, guest speakers included two prominent local political consultants who appear on a statewide TV show, and two members of the Green Independent Party, who explained the dynamics of third-party politics. In the unit's hands-on component, students staffed voter-registration tables in public areas around Portland, taking the opportunity to interview voters and hand out surveys about voting behavior.

Ultimately, the King middle schoolers had a chance to demonstrate what they had learned by collaborating to organize a school-wide mock election. The kids teamed up into subcommittees responsible for making ballot boxes, registering voters, creating and distributing posters, and monitoring voting booths. "We made the whole school into an electoral college," explained social studies teacher Carol Nylen. "We had enough classrooms for the fifty states plus Washington, DC."

The teachers designated the largest homeroom as California and the smaller homerooms as the Dakotas, Alaska, Vermont, Washington, DC, Hawaii, and Rhode Island. The sixth graders made a huge map that they hung outside the cafeteria so students could see which state their homeroom represented. The ballots asked voters to weigh in on a new president, U.S. senator, U.S. representative, and five statewide referendum issues. After the vote, using what they'd learned in math, students analyzed the data, breaking down the results by gender, grade, and state, and following the real-world national election, comparing it to statewide and national results.

As challenging, enlightening, and rewarding as this level

of integration is for students, these experiences can be equally revolutionary for teachers, many of whom have been as uninspired as their students by the old-fashioned drill-and-skill methods still prevalent today. Yet a culture and ethic built around Deeper Learning offers the opportunity to work together, with other teachers, to connect students' learning experiences through a genuinely multidisciplinary approach. Pockets of time—short or long, formal or informal, before or after school—afforded to the teachers for this purpose are invaluable and have to be institutionally and structurally supported by the leadership. It creates the aforementioned PLCs: a situation in which professional development is peer-led and the topics are collegially agreed upon. This type of space allows teachers to continually work on issues of common concern, share effective strategies, and generally think collaboratively about how to create the best possible learning experiences for every student.

The result, as we witnessed on our travels to these schools, is that every teacher has the necessary tools (primarily time and knowledge) to develop their own skills in the multiple roles we know that all teachers play. Consequently, in this type of empowered, supportive professional community, while no less work is being done (much time is spent planning, engaging students, and reflecting), we noticed that teachers seem to maintain their own motivation and develop an organic confidence and competence in their ability to guide students. All of this (most especially the high level of autonomy), in fact, ends up mirroring many of the skills and traits that teachers hope students will develop themselves—being self-directed, critical thinkers who problem solve, communicate effectively, and collaborate productively. It is, in essence, the engagement of teachers in this ongoing deep learning process that in turn enables them to cultivate Deeper Learning for their students.

PLCS, ASSESSMENTS, AND SETTING HIGH EXPECTATIONS

To best ignite kids' drive to learn, teachers must not only engage them through their interests, but show them as clearly as possible how their efforts can help them develop useful skills. This is the main guidance in Grant Wiggins and Jay McTighe's insightful book, *Understanding by Design*. Their message: learning begins when teachers clearly identify the reasons behind the instruction, and more precisely, what students will need to be able to know and do upon completion of a unit, project, or course.[6] In all of the schools we visited, we noted that teachers make sure to clarify the learning goals, in terms of the content knowledge and skills they want students to acquire, as well as the assessments they will use. As Wiggins and McTighe contend: "The first question for curriculum writers is not: What will we teach and when should we teach it? Rather the initial question for curriculum development must be goal-focused: Having learned key content, what will students be able to do with it?"[7]

This method strongly implies that teachers will hold high expectations for students, which, in fact, as researchers have shown, is in itself an exceptionally effective teaching tactic, as long as teachers also make sure to provide adequate support.[8] This dynamic has been called the Pygmalion effect, a reference to the ancient narrative by Ovid about a sculptor who fell in love with the statue he had created. The implication is that people can influence others by projecting an image onto them that in some cases has little to do with reality. Research suggests that teachers often create self-fulfilling prophesies with their students, as the students interpret subtle and sometimes not-so-subtle messages. The phenomenon was first revealed in a 1968 study by Robert Rosenthal and Lenore Jacobson, which inspired a great deal of follow-up research. The two psychologists found that by influencing teachers' expectations about their students, telling them, erroneously, that some had performed exceptionally well on an intelligence test, teachers could even affect the development of the students' future IQs.[9] (Teachers unconsciously invested more time and energy in the students for whom they had the highest expectations.)

What's particularly worrisome is that teachers apparently make such decisions about students' capacity all the time, whether guided by researchers or not, affecting the students' futures sometimes for the most unjust of reasons. A recent longitudinal study of ten cities by educational psychologist Nicole S. Sorhagen at Temple University suggests the effects of teacher expectations vary according to the students' family income. Writing in the *Journal of Educational Psychology*, Sorhagen concluded that:

> Teachers' inaccurate expectations in first grade predicted students' math, reading comprehension, vocabulary knowledge, and verbal reasoning standardized test scores at age 15. Significant interactions between students' family income and teachers' misperceptions of students' math and language skills were found, such that teachers' over- and underestimation of abilities had a stronger impact

on students from lower income families than on students
from more affluent homes.[10]

Common among the teachers we interviewed was a general awareness of these potential minefields, even when they
didn't know chapter and verse of the research, and a conscious
focus on communicating high expectations to *all* of their students. At MC^2, one particularly powerful way that teachers
accomplish this is in their grading system, by which students
must achieve "mastery" in order to earn high school credit.
Mastery in this case signifies greater than or equal to 90 percent in grades nine and ten, and greater than or equal to 70
percent in grades eleven and twelve, on each state standard.
The mastery-learning system was originated by Benjamin
Bloom, circa 1968, when he suggested that setting such standards might help reduce student achievement gaps.[11] And,
indeed, the message sent to students is strict, clear, and inspiring: they aren't allowed or expected ever to coast. The choices
are, essentially, an A or an F, and nothing in between, with
the expectation that students will strive for the A.

About half of MC^2 students fulfill all mastery requirements
in the first three years. If a student doesn't master a benchmark on a specific project, he or she is not required to retake
the course, but rather, the next teachers in line work with
the student to make sure it's mastered in subsequent work. In
the years since Bloom introduced the concept, other researchers have presented evidence suggesting that the system indeed
leads to higher achievement. Even so, relatively few schools
have adopted the practice. While advocates of mastery learning say it can be accomplished with as little as a 10 to 20 percent increase in teachers' time, many teachers contend they

are already working at full capacity.[12] Yet as evidenced by the model schools we draw from here, it appears that school design may hold the key to transitioning to different, more demanding evaluation systems, like mastery learning. While a traditionally structured school day and common teaching and learning methods may render this sort of grading structure overly cumbersome, a school designed more flexibly, such as those we describe here, could by design provide the necessary support teachers need to adopt more complex, thoughtful forms of assessing student learning.

In each case we observed, teachers demonstrated a variety of other ways to communicate high and specific expectations of their students. Many take care to display models of high-quality work by previous students before their class undertakes a new project. At the Science Leadership Academy, for instance, Diana Laufenberg begins her project on voting and elections by providing copies of well-designed interview questions from previous years so the students can refer to them as they come up with their own questions.

Students embarking on new ventures routinely are given a rubric—a scoring tool with a set of criteria for each project they undertake. Teachers told us that they believed the rubrics not only made the students more accountable, but continually reminded both teachers and students of the aims of the assignment. They also motivated students to ask questions throughout the process.

"Learning targets" play a similar role. These are conceptual questions and goals that are prominently displayed or repeated by teachers as part of their instruction. At King Middle School, for instance, eighth graders building their wind turbines can look to a poster on the wall, with its clear mission statement: "I know how to use experimentation and the design process to create a wind turbine that meets specific design criteria and generates electricity." Moreover, at the end of each class, some teachers informally assess what students have learned by having them fill out "exit tickets," answering a question about what they have just learned. Teachers review the tickets each day to see whether they need to review the material during the next class before continuing with a new lesson.

The Casco Bay High teachers use learning targets in similar ways. The chemistry class's overall learning target for its unit on fossil fuels is: "I will be able to describe the impact of coal on our environment." Students are also expected to be able to offer answers to the question, "How do we resolve our dependence on fossil fuels?" In learning about the role of chemical elements and reactions in affecting climate change, other learning targets include: "I will be able to describe the carbon cycle and its importance in moving carbon dioxide in and out of the atmosphere," "I will be able to describe the greenhouse effect," and "I will be able to describe how coal is formed and the different types of coal."

LEARNING IS A JOURNEY

To be sure, of all the integrated projects we learned of, Casco Bay's Junior Journey was determinedly bold and complex. We offer you details about it, once again, not as a formula that must be followed to the letter, but as a glimpse of what is possible, including the way many students respond to some extremely high expectations.

The project began as a stand-alone endeavor: a kind of extended field trip unrelated to the rest of the academic year. Since then, Susan McCray told us, teachers realized that they could build whole academic units around the week of travel, with the carrot of the upcoming adventurous journey providing extra motivation to study. At the same time, students got real-world practice in collaboration, problem solving, and creativity by participating in the necessary fund-raising efforts.

Beginning in the sophomore year, each future Junior Journey participant is responsible for helping to raise money for the trip, and also for contributing to his or her own travel expenses. With half of the student population coming from families in poverty, the teachers understand that not every one of them can afford the costs of the trip. Yet it becomes a part of the learning experience to be responsible for something, so even kids who are eligible for free lunches at school are expected to pay at least $125, which they have more than a year to raise. "The expectation is that it's up to the kids, not the parents," says Nancy Hagstrom. "Most kids figure it out, but we tell them to come talk to us if they're having trouble. There are some students who end up making contracts to do small jobs at school, earning $10 or so a week."

Each year, two sophomores step up to coordinate fund-raising activities for the entire class, while other students volunteer for specific tasks, such as advertising and using social media to publicize fund-raising events. In crew, or advisory period, students brainstorm ideas and plan raffles, yard sales, bottle drives, and dance marathons. The strong school community that, as with all of our model schools, has been established from the start of freshman year makes the fund-raising work easier by motivating kids to work hard out of a sense of responsibility toward their school as an institution and to each other. At the same time, the school's increasing renown in the broader community has made the job of fund-raising somewhat easier, especially since, in recent years, a few major donors have supported the journey with large grants.

After eight years in Portland, Casco Bay High School today has exceptional support from its community, although this wasn't always the case. The city has two other larger high schools with loyal followings and long histories, and McCray and Hagstrom vividly remember how, when Casco Bay first opened, the local newspaper went on the offensive.

"We struggled with a reputation for being fluffy nature lovers who wouldn't provide any academic rigor," said McCray. "Part of it was that people were scared of the new model," recalled Hagstrom. "There was definitely also a sense that we were stealing resources from other schools, which, of course, wasn't true. It's classic to be afraid of what you don't know, and we are so, so different. It took a few years to prove that we were doing a good job, and that in our different way, our kids were getting good scores, going to college, and really enjoying school." Today the school has many admirers of its focus on a strong community, relevant and adventurous learning, and well-integrated subjects, and there are long waiting lists of students seeking to enroll. As one Casco Bay student told us, after transferring in as a sophomore, "At my other school, you just learn from the text and you forget everything. Here you build on everything you learn and you retain it because it's important to you."

On their journey to West Virginia in the spring, the students followed what has been an established routine of combining interviewing with community service, which in this case was helping to build houses for homeless families. The hammering and sawing took up the mornings, with afternoons reserved for exploring the area, making observations, taking photographs, and, in the end, sitting down with families who would eventually take up residence in the Habitat housing to ask questions they had practiced in advance.

The students worked in teams, trading off the jobs of interviewing, photographing, taking notes, and audiotaping the interviews. By then, they were used to working in groups, although this exercise tested that skill as never before. Many students began the week feeling anxious about whether they could rise to the challenge. As Hagstrom told us, "One student who comes off as so incredibly competent and composed just broke down one night and shared how fearful she was about not knowing what she would do when she got down here."

Teachers don't directly participate in the interviews, although they are close by to provide support. No student is barred from the journeys, despite widely varying abilities, some medical issues, and an occasional spotty behavioral record. (Fifteen percent of Casco Bay's students have learning challenges that qualify them for special education.) Before each trip begins, every student must sign a discipline contract, and theoretically, anyone breaking the rules will be sent home at his or her parents' expense. To date, however, this has never happened, Hagstrom told us. Instead, she and McCray say they have witnessed remarkable personal transformations on the journeys.

"One year, one of my advisees was really learning disabled, and could barely read or write," Hagstrom recalled. "He had always been a behavioral problem in school, wandering the hall and ending up in the principal's office. He had ADHD and some major learning problems and a rough home life that complicated things. But once we arrived, in this case in New Orleans, he was in his element. We were building houses for [Hurricane] Katrina families, and he was amazing. The construction people recognized it and gave him leadership responsibilities. He was so happy that he chose to continue working rather than go on the fun activities we had planned. I think he realized he could do something constructive after high school on that trip."

Teachers make sure to give the kids plenty of time to discuss and reflect on the novel experiences they encounter each day. Of the 2011 trip, teachers told us that the dinners in West Virginia were animated by conversation about the people the students had interviewed. One team of students, for instance, had interviewed a homeless woman who revealed that she needed a new house for herself and her children because she had left a husband who had beaten her. "We never expected that," said one student, who added that she felt she had to try hard "to be a listening presence instead of an invading presence to get her story. That's what Ms. McCray taught us before we went on the journey."

After dinner, the student teams reported to various rooms to review the work they had done that day. One group, huddled over a laptop, looked at the photographs they had taken, while another read over the interview notes. Teachers circulated among the groups, prodding them with questions like "What is the thread of the story so far, and what will you ask next?" As Nancy Hagstrom sees it, the point of the Appalachia trip isn't necessarily to familiarize students with poverty—sadly, most of her students already understand it all too well. Instead, she said, it's meant to deepen kids' concepts of culture and community, particularly in unfamiliar parts of America, and, more importantly, to give them a chance to step out of their own lives to help others, which she believes is a deeply influential experience.

Indeed, Hagstrom noted, one of her students recently returned to West Virginia to do volunteer work during the summer. For most of the rest, she said, "Our kids come back understanding that they can make a difference. For some, that means a difference in their own lives—they begin to really engage with their academics, for example, or simply show up at school more consistently. For others, it means to make a difference in their school community, to connect with others in their classes, to lend a hand, to volunteer to help with school events."

Each year, the trips also reliably help build stronger bonds between the students themselves and between the students and teachers, said McCray. "The teachers become real people as they share experiences with the students," she said. "When we're back in the classroom, there's another level of respect that has developed between the students and the teachers." That's fortuitous, considering that some of the project's most challenging work lays ahead.

Once the West Virginia travelers returned to Maine, each one of them wrote up a full oral history of the West Virginian resident interviewed by his or her group. Working as a team, the group then created a concise, three-minute narrative of that person's life, integrating elements from each student's oral history. The students then used audio equipment to record themselves reading their parts of the script, and they pieced the story together with photographs and segments of their interviews with West Virginians. Students spent several hours of class time preparing their stories, working individually and in teams. McCray devoted her English periods to helping them draft, combine, and revise the scripts. Then, in groups, the students took turns reading each other's drafts aloud.

As we observed this process, we overheard several encouraging comments, such as: "We need to use your introduction; it's beautiful!" and "I loved the way you wrote the story of how they rescued that woman." It was clear to us that the kids had emotionally connected with the people they had interviewed and were intent on honoring them for what they repeatedly referred to as the gifts of their stories.

McCray told us about one of her students who was "transformed" by interviewing a Vietnam veteran whose wife had left him after fifty years of marriage. The student's father had passed away a few years earlier, and so she was fascinated by how the man had weathered his loss, how he managed to be so resilient. McCray recalls seeing the student return from the interview, "glowing, in tears—and I can still see her, sitting on the floor in my classroom, staring at the screen, tortured about how to get [the veteran's] story right." The student later submitted an essay about her experience as part of a college application. Her acceptance letter came with a handwritten note from the admissions officer, saying how much the essay had moved her.

For McCray, the most important payoff of sending the kids out, in their role of "documentarians," to ask intimate questions of strangers, is that "it gets them thinking about the quintessentially real-world question of how they want to live their own lives. You're going in to learn, and try to get a story, and then your job is to make meaning of that story. In the process, you can't help but realize that life has meaning, and that your own life can and will have meaning and you have the ability to craft and shape that meaning as you go. And it's perfect timing, during the junior year, as they're just beginning to think about their lives outside home. We talk about giving them career awareness. This is more profound."

Ultimately, the Casco Bay juniors produced 15 three-minute documentaries, linked together and presented at an evening event at the Salt Gallery in downtown Portland, an institute for documentary studies. More than two hundred people attended, including parents, students, local volunteers from Portland's Habitat for Humanity chapter, and other Portland residents who were intrigued by the press releases. The evening included a performance of bluegrass tunes by student and staff musicians, and ended with two students singing "Country Road."

McCray then shipped off DVDs to West Virginia, and the following week, the Habitat Volunteer Center hosted a gathering for the interviewees, volunteers, and other community members. "The Habitat coordinator sent me a note afterward about how she was in tears watching it, since it revealed all these things about folks—like their resiliency and their strength—that she hadn't really known even after working with them for years," McCray said.

McCray, one of Casco Bay's founding teachers, and the initial mastermind of the Junior Journey, has always been creative in designing her teaching projects. Before she came to Portland in 2005, she worked as an instructor for Outward Bound, an experience she credits for her skill in encouraging kids to see learning as an adventure. Her first teaching job was at a public school in the South Bronx in New York City, where she led kids on expeditions that included climbing ropes in the rigging of a tall ship docked in the harbor of Lower Manhattan, and rowing large boats down the Hudson River.

"If you want to change a young person's life, that means providing opportunities for real experiences," she said. (When we last spoke with her, she was researching a potential expedition to visit residents of Sandy Hook in New Jersey, following the 2012 storms.) McCray is nonetheless adamant that you don't need to travel ten hours by bus and spend $40,000 to engage with the real world, or make education relevant. "Just look at your curriculum and what you have to teach, and find what matters," she advised. "Find something the student wants to produce that has some meaning. It doesn't have to be a big expedition. It could be something as simple as a letter to the editor. The trick is to find what matters and do what you can."

A BLUEPRINT FOR DEEPER LEARNING

- Evidence supports the fact that learning becomes more efficient—with faster and deeper retention—when material is personally relevant and subjects are integrated. Even so, most conventional schools still teach subjects in isolation.

- Teachers can make learning more meaningful and effective by integrating subjects and connecting them to real-world problems, rather than presenting them in a compartmentalized manner only focused on the knowledge and not the application of it.

- Teachers who clearly communicate high expectations for students are better positioned to empower students to rise up to meet them.

- Professional learning communities enable teachers to integrate curricula, with time built into their daily schedules for planning and collaboration. It is absolutely essential that administrators (at the school, district, and state levels) clear the path for this to happen by providing support to teachers.

4

REACH
NETWORK BEYOND SCHOOL WALLS

"In an average school, you just study for a test, and that's
it. But at MC², you're excited to retain the information."
—Andrea Lane, former student at MC² STEM High School
in Cleveland, Ohio

WIDENED HORIZONS

*The Science Leadership Academy in Philadelphia is housed in
a retrofitted office building that has seen better days. There is
no gym and no auditorium. But every day, the students walk
just three blocks down to the Franklin Institute, an enormous
nineteenth-century building that houses a world-renowned science museum named after Benjamin Franklin. The kids scram-
ble up the broad stone steps, past giant Gothic columns and a
majestic glass door, into an intellectual wonderland.*

*In a rare yet highly beneficial arrangement for students
at SLA, which opened in 2006, the museum joined with the
Philadelphia School District as a powerful founding partner for*

the school. Today, in just one of the many fruits of the collabo-
ration, SLA students attend "mini-courses" taught by Franklin
Institute scholars, with topics ranging from immunology to as-
tronomy to computer programming to product design. The sub-
jects are brought to life with hundreds of hands-on, state-of-the
art exhibits, including a giant walk-through heart that illus-
trates the circulation system, a climb-aboard steam engine that
helps teach transportation mechanics, and a simulated Space
Command earth-orbit research station. A chemical engineer em-
ployed by the Franklin Institute teaches a popular class in fo-
rensic science, in which students use ultraviolet light to examine
fake blood splattered on a wall. Programming experts tutor kids
in developing their own computer animations and smart phone
applications.

The Science Leadership Academy serves approximately 480
students, who come to the school from all over Philadelphia.
Nearly 70 percent of them are students of color and half come
from families in poverty. But thanks in large part to the school's
strategic partnership with the Franklin Institute, its students have
been beating the odds, and more. SLA students outperform the
district by far on state tests, with 83 percent proficient or above
in math and 85 percent proficient or above in reading. In 2012,
SLA had a 93 percent graduation rate, compared to 55 percent
for the district and 83 percent for the state.[1]

THE POWER OF PARTNERS

A key strength of schools throughout the country that truly
embody Deeper Learning is their strategic use of partnerships
to support their vision for students. Partnerships between

schools and businesses and community groups are nothing new in the United States, but the reality of these budget-crunching (and -cutting) times means there is a lot of new incentive—and even necessity—for schools to supplement their resources and reach.

While tens of thousands of schools have created an affiliation with some sort of partner, many make the mistake of treating them as outsiders held at arm's length, whose role is limited to writing checks or sponsoring interns as glorified clerks, or sending staff members to the school's career days. As a result, there's plenty of room for such collaborations to fail in contributing to genuine learning.

In contrast, by reaching out to their communities in creative and unconventional ways, Deeper Learning schools tap resources, engage mentors, and, ultimately, significantly widen their students' horizons. While schools of all types can engage in these alliances, the trend has been particularly productive when it comes to schools oriented toward science, technology, engineering, and math, the STEM subjects, in which American kids are so infamously falling behind their industrialized-nation peers. Innovative partnerships—with museums, high-tech corporations, and colleges—not only offer kids sophisticated resources, such as industrial labs, that ordinary schools could rarely if ever provide on their own, they also provide real-world excitement that's inspiring a new wave of students to explore STEM-centered careers.

While SLA has set a high bar with its bold networking formula, MC^2 in Cleveland has the most far-reaching alliances of the STEM schools we discuss in this book. Back in 2007, the Cleveland School District worked out an "embedded partnership" with two large institutions: Great Lakes

Science Center, site of the NASA Glenn Visitor Center, and the General Electric International Lighting Division, both of which today serve as hosts for MC^2 students. Ninth graders attend their classes at the museum, in a remodeled gallery in the basement, while tenth graders report each day to the GE International Lighting Division's corporate campus. (GE charges $1 in rent per year on a four-year lease agreement for half of a building that originally was designed as a research facility but was shut down due to downsizing about a decade ago.) Today, MC^2 also has a third campus: as of 2013, juniors and seniors attend school at Cleveland State University. These students spend most of their academic time fulfilling internships with high-tech industrial partners and attending college classes.

To date, GE has invested more than $860,000 in employee-volunteer time, GE Foundation Grants, STEM internship salaries, and equipment and supplies in the school, according to Andrea Timan, GE Lighting's community relations manager and the liaison to MC^2. "GE Lighting's partnership with MC^2 STEM High School is the most elaborate school-business partnership in the nation," Timan told us. "There are a lot of corporations that are able to donate large contributions to students, host great intern or co-op programs, and that volunteer, but the collaboration and the embedding of a high school into the world headquarters of GE Lighting is the largest partnership I know of."

GE Lighting's hopes for the alliance are equally grand. STEM schools such as MC^2, together with their partners, "are going to have a large impact on improving the future economy," Timan predicted. Not only will they boost math and science skills, she said, but they'll prepare students to

work in teams, to think more creatively, and to be more innovative from a much earlier age. "The real-world experience will also reduce the learning curve upon entry to the
work force," she said. "Once students enter the work force,
they will be more effective to their business from prior experience and understanding the reality and pace of 'corporate life.'"

The GE Lighting partnership is a particularly vivid example of a growing national movement for businesses to be
more involved in public schools. For both the businesses and
schools, the motivations to affiliate have arguably never been
keener. While, as we've mentioned, schools are scrambling
to supplement budgets in an era of harsh funding cutbacks,
business leaders worry that the scrambling schools are failing
to prepare students for the modern work force.

That's why, for instance, elsewhere in Ohio, Cincinnati Bell
has rebuilt the Robert A. Taft School into Taft Information
Technology High School, while California business leaders, led by former Qualcomm executive Gary Jacobs, joined
together in 2000 to help create High Tech High. Elsewhere,
other schools engage in ongoing, even if less robust, partnerships, often to support specific projects. To prepare students for their Junior Journey from Casco Bay High School
in Portland, Maine, for instance, a project described in the
previous chapter, teachers reach out to local businesses and
nonprofit organizations. To enhance students' understanding of Appalachian culture, the teachers developed a partnership with the 317 Main Street Music Community Center, a
nonprofit organization based in Yarmouth, Maine. As part
of the preparations for the trip, the center provided two staff
members, offering support to the humanities course, help-

ing students understand the development of bluegrass music, and playing songs in class to demonstrate the powerful role of music in sustaining regional culture. Simultaneously, the Salt Institute for Documentary Studies, another nonprofit based in Portland, collaborated to help the Casco Bay teachers train students in interviewing and photography skills. Their instructors modeled good interviewing techniques and engaged students in thinking about questions such as, "How do you show you are open to another person?" and "How do you sit across the table from a person and listen and form another question to get the essence of his or her life story?" In later sessions, the students took turns practicing by interviewing the Salt Institute director, and finally heading out into Portland to interview people they met on the street.

At King Middle School, also in Portland, students have teamed up with city officials and the Gulf of Maine Research Institute (GMRI), a local nonprofit marine science center, to brainstorm tactics to control local invasive plants. In San Diego, High Tech High students have worked with the San Diego Blood Bank to design informational DVDs about blood-related health issues and build dioramas with embedded video displays to publicize the need for blood donors.

The common thread in all of these joint ventures is that students are constantly connecting with people and resources outside of the school walls, enriching each student's learning experiences in unique ways. Cultural and scientific institutions, nonprofit organizations, and even for-profit businesses provide the schools with novel and meaningful opportunities for learning, while also making what they learn inside the classroom more relevant to the wider world. Kids rarely need to ask why they are learning something in class, since they have so many opportunities to see the same knowledge and skills used in professional settings. In particular, students see firsthand how the Deeper Learning skills that their teachers are coaching them to develop—problem solving, critical thinking, creativity, effective communication, and collaboration—work to their advantage in the adult worlds of business, academia, and community activism.

These innovative partnerships are particularly vital for schools, like the eight explored here, that serve high proportions of children from families in poverty, in that they provide "social capital"—edifying experiences and professional contacts that affluent children often take for granted.[2] For kids whose parents lack the time and money to haul them around to endless after-school activities and high-priced enrichment programs, a school's ties with a museum, organization, or other entity can fast-track a child's discovery of his or her natural talents. Opportunities to work with and learn from museum scholars, inventors, and corporate leaders can be life changing. The deep involvement that members of partner organizations develop with the principals, teachers, and students creates a shared sense of responsibility for the students' success, which in turn leads to a willingness to invest more time, money, and energy. As Whitney Owens, vice president for education at Great Lakes Science Center, told us: "We try to give the students any opportunities we can. We feel like MC[2] is our school, too."

At the schools we visited, that pride and care manifests as everything from physical resources, including sophisticated labs and museum exhibits, to enthusiastic "buddies," including the GE Lighting, NASA, and Franklin Institute professionals who volunteer their time to tutor and guide their adopted schools' students, to a range of other mind-expanding adventures that we'll describe in the following pages.

LOCATION, LOCATION, LOCATION

Because MC^2 freshmen take classes on-site at Great Lakes Science Center, one of their founding partners, their teachers can liven up their physics, math, and engineering classes and deepen students' knowledge by means of hundreds of hands-on exhibits relating to electricity, light, and space travel. Some of the most popular items on display include a moon rock, John Glenn's space suit, Skylab 3, and a wind turbine that provides 7 percent of the museum's energy. All represent riches that most other budget-stretched public schools would justifiably envy, and which most students, in well-resourced schools or not, wouldn't have at their fingertips. Most importantly, this type of knowledge access is fertile ground for Deeper Learning, giving students the chance to work with real-world scenarios and phenomena.

"Having the Science Center all around you gives teachers so many opportunities to grab student interest and build on it," says Phil Bucur, who teaches engineering in custom-built classrooms housed in a former museum gallery that overlooks the North Coast Harbor district.

These kinds of opportunities are an all-too-rare occurrence in a city like Cleveland. MC^2's student body is drawn entirely from the Cleveland Metropolitan School District, Ohio's second-largest school district and also one of the nation's poorest, with 83 percent of families at the poverty level and two thousand students who are homeless.[3]

The same feeling of doors opening to new worlds infuses Philadelphia's Science Leadership Academy, located in another economically strapped metropolis, yet where the resources of one of the nation's leading museums exponentially increase a teacher's means to inspire students. To boot, every SLA student and staff member is provided with a family membership to the Franklin Institute, with free access to all permanent exhibits, even outside of school hours. This collection includes favorites like the popular Sky Bike, on which visitors can ride a high tightrope, and the distinguished Fels Planetarium.

On one of our visits to MC^2, Bucur illustrated how teachers can integrate their curricula with Great Lakes Science Center exhibits as he began a unit on electricity by showing a group of students the properties of a Tesla ball—a kind of electrical transformer—on display at the museum. He asked one of the freshmen to put his hands on the ball, after which the boy jumped back, his hair standing on end, and the rest of the class exploded in laughter. Bucur then picked another student as his guinea pig, asking her to hold a fluorescent bulb. Next, he passed her the Tesla ball. Electricity moved through the girl's body to turn the bulb on, eliciting *oohs* and *aahs* from her classmates. Bucur concluded the demonstration by pairing up the students and directing them to use a multimeter to measure and record the electrical output of each other's bodies.

"When I use an exhibit here, it doesn't always need to exactly relate to the lesson of the day," Bucur told us later. "I have the students produce a regular journal of their experiences in the Science Center. If I see that an exhibit sparks their interest, I'll revise my curriculum to take advantage of that. You can't be so regimented in your lesson plan if you want to turn students on to science and technology." A willingness on the part of teachers, and support on the part of school leadership, to facilitate flexible, dynamic learning experiences is an ingredient for successful Deeper Learning to occur.

While freshmen explore the Science Center, the sophomores, as we've noted, attend class at a second site, based at the corporate campus of GE's International Lighting Division. It's an excellent place for them to gain an appreciation of what it's like in the professional world, and a particularly exciting world at that. The adult-like status the kids enjoy encourages them to develop the "academic mindset"[4] that is so key to motivating them to take responsibility for their own learning.

The tenth graders report to class by signing in and showing their ID cards, just like regular GE Lighting employees. And the similarities don't end there. Once they pass through the gates, the kids work alongside GE Lighting engineers in workshops supplied with cutting-edge production machinery. At noon, they eat lunch together in the corporate cafeteria.

The center of activity for sophomores studying at General Electric is the Fab Lab (short for Fabrication Laboratory)—a mobile workshop stocked with computers running user-friendly software, with laser cutters that make 2-D and 3-D structures, a high-resolution milling machine that makes circuit boards and precision parts, and a large wood router for manufacturing furniture.

MC^2 was the first public school in America to get access to this high-tech inventor's playground. It did so through yet another partnership, this time with the Center for Bits & Atoms at the Massachusetts Institute of Technology, where professor Neil Gershenfeld and colleagues created the Fab Lab concept in the 1990s. MC² principal Jeff McClellan said the school had received $100,000 in grant money for a traditional science laboratory, with microscopes and chemistry equipment. He decided instead to use the funds to purchase the small production line, which fits in better with MC²'s focus on design, and lets students practice their problem-solving and collaboration skills on more authentic, industrial-grade fabrication. Since then, the kids have produced such sophisticated products as a six-legged robot and a working artificial heart.

On a wintry afternoon, we watched sophomores using computers to design Koch snowflakes—an example of a complex geometrical concept called a fractal (in layperson's terms, a detailed pattern that repeats itself)—after which they donned safety goggles and used the production equipment to build models of the snowflakes out of cut Masonite, a type of hardboard, and add LED lights. They worked with a keen sense of purpose, since they were approaching a deadline to contribute their finished snowflakes to a corporate campus Winterfest display.[5] And while the students devoted many hours to the project, it carried a big payback for them. McClellan believes the Fab Lab practice helps raise students' math test scores, as they apply mathematical concepts and principles to design, prototyping, and fabrication.

The MC² students aren't limited to working in the Fab Lab; they also have access to the main GE labs as they work on their sophomore project, a challenging, hands-on seminar course that draws on all they learn throughout the year. GE scientists, engineers, and managers guide students through the curriculum, working alongside them and adding real-world expertise in applied technology—a world unknown to most if not all of their traditionally trained teachers. In the project, students replicate the GE Lighting employees' activities, as they simulate corporate development of a brand new product, of their own invention, involving LED lights. They form into teams, which they refer to as "companies," and take the process from an initial idea to a fabricated prototype to a final product with a business and marketing plan.

The GE Lighting employees coach the students through every stage of the product development process, challenging them as to how their invention—be it a robot or a solar-powered cell phone charger or illuminated jewelry—might be used and who the customers would be, and making sure they understand the engineering principles underlying their designs. The student teams eventually use the Fab Lab to produce sample products, with their GE Lighting coaches monitoring and troubleshooting along the way. After that, the student companies consult with corporate management and marketing professionals to come up with a business plan for each of their ideas. This latter stage of the project is particularly important in developing the students' persuasive communication skills, with opportunities to practice interviewing and presenting with people who do just that in their jobs all day long.

Each team has a hypothetical budget of $1,000,000 to bring their product to market. While the students are usually initially impressed by their theoretical wealth, they often change their minds once they start calculating the real-world expenses involved in designing and marketing a new product. We sat in on one of the seminars, during which a GE Lighting marketing expert was prodding a team that was developing a belt adorned with an LED light they had designed.

"How will you promote it? Where will you advertise?" the GE Lighting employee asked the group.

One student suggested recruiting a rap star to endorse the product.

"Okay, that's a good idea," the GE Lighting instructor responded. "But do you want to spend all your money on a single celebrity or are there other ways to promote the belt light?"

Two eager students interrupted each other to answer.

"We should go to clubs and show them to people," said one.

Offered another: "We could have kiosks at clubs where people could see the belts and try them on."

The group debated these ideas for a few minutes, after which the GE Lighting employee reassured them: "This is just like the meetings I have. Members of my team sit around talking through these same kinds of issues and we use our spreadsheets to make sure we're keeping within a budget, just like you are doing now."

The grand finale of the sophomore project is a trade show presentation, in which student teams show off and explain their products to an audience of GE Lighting employees. By the end of the experience, the kids not only have put into practice every one of their Deeper Learning skills, but they have gotten an inside view of what it's like to work as a professional engineer.

THE BENEFITS OF BUDDIES

On a late September morning in 2011, in a large conference room on the GE Lighting campus, half a dozen MC^2 tenth graders took turns interviewing corporate employees for three minutes at a time. The students had been given profiles of the employees, and made their way to the ones working in the fields that most interested them, such as management, engineering, or information technology. Andrea Timan, a GE Lighting public relations manager, refers to this annual ritual as "speed dating"—and, in fact, these conversations are explicitly intended to lead to long-term relationships. At the start of the students' sophomore year, each of them is expected to choose a corporate "buddy" to advise him or her on a major upcoming project, and, in many cases, offer tutoring, friendship, advice, and, ultimately, even professional references or a job. These partnerships can be, and often are, life changing, and not just for the students.

In an interview with Edutopia.org, GE Lighting physicist Gary Allen told of an awkward sophomore he met in 2009 who initially confided that he was planning to drop out because he couldn't keep up with the schoolwork. Allen struck a bargain: he'd tutor the boy throughout the year if he committed to staying in school. Allen did more than his part; besides tutoring the boy, he met with his parents, teachers, and school officials to guide him throughout the year. The boy stuck it out, and graduated in 2012 with the school's first graduating class. Allen, who attended the ceremony, said: "The hugs from family and the tears in his mom's eyes are memories that will stay with me forever."[6]

Allen's experience is echoed in research that shows that close mentoring and support of students is key in reducing the rate of high school dropouts.[7] This is what makes the GE Lighting speed-dating system for buddies so important.

On their first meeting with their potential buddies, most of the sophomores we observed at first seemed shy, avoiding eye contact and answering questions as briefly as possible. This wasn't a big surprise, considering how little the two groups seemed to have in common, at least initially. The

GE Lighting workers, after all, were almost without exception middle-aged, white, and relatively affluent, in contrast to the MC^2 students, who were, of course, young teens, with about 80 percent of them African American, and mostly from low-income families. After just a few minutes, however, the GE Lighting employees, who by then had been through several similar meetings, succeeded in breaking the ice, and the room filled with chatter. By the end of the hour, each of the sophomores had identified a buddy, and each new pair had set up a time for a follow-up meeting.

The buddies meet regularly—twice a month or more—throughout the school year. "We talk about everyday life, the projects at the school, some of my activities, our families, how our weekends went," said one student, who was paired up with an engineer specializing in infrared lighting. The power of these mentoring relationships is much bigger than the personal relationships and bonds that are formed amid all of the learning taking place; students are simultaneously exposed to the dynamics involved in building professional relationships, allowing them to develop their own understanding of skill-based, collegial environments.

The GE Lighting employee-volunteers, who have included high-level managers and inventors—among them Dr. Nick Holonyak Jr., the father of the LED light bulb—often go to great lengths for their buddies. One engineer, for instance, let his student partner shadow him as he moved through his working day. ("It's like an Apple store," the student later told us of watching his buddy interact with his lab mates. "Out front everything is white and gleaming, but if you go in the back, everybody is working incredibly hard.") Another GE Lighting mentor, who had graduated from West Point, made it his business to get his buddy into the academy as well, an effort that turned into a multi-year campaign, which the GE Lighting employee called "Operation Get John into West Point."[8] During that time, the GE employee spoke to the boy's parents, introduced him to other local West Point alumni, and taught him how to buff up his high school resume with community service, athletics, and other activities that would help qualify him for admission. (When we checked with Andrea Timan in the fall of 2013, the student had not yet applied to West Point, although his mentor was keeping up the campaign, while also reaching out to other students who might be good candidates.)

Toward the end of the sophomore year, GE Lighting volunteers focus on preparing the tenth graders for their junior-year job internship, walking them through the processes of resume writing and interviewing, and even building up a professional wardrobe. A formal practice session is held each spring, when each student has a one-on-one interview with a GE Lighting employee as final preparation for the internship interview. Yet even after the buddy system officially ends, many pairs have gone on to meet informally through the student's junior and senior year, supplementing the guidance they receive with subjects such as how to pick a college, how to choose a major, and where to look for a job.

Once again, while all of our eight model schools reach outside classroom walls in some way to take advantage of resources in their communities, MC^2 has developed particularly strong and integrated partnerships. The GE Lighting buddy system is just one example of its imaginative and ambitious use of its partners' personnel. Over at Great Lakes Science Center, the school recruits volunteers among NASA employees to serve as tutors, mentors, and occasional classroom teachers for the freshmen who attend engineering classes there.

In particular, NASA engineers play a key role in the school's capstone project on bridges, described in chapter three. As the freshmen design the model bridges they're assigned to build at the end of the unit, the NASA experts step in to give the project an extra dose of authenticity. The students bring their bridges to the center's lab, where the professional engineers help them mount them on "shaker tables" to test their structural integrity. The engineers video-record these tests, just as they would with their own prototypes, after which each student group sits down with one of the adults to consider the results. "As the students review the video, they actually see how the engineering concepts of stress, strength, and structural multipliers relate to load-bearing designs, and the engineers talk with them about how they use math and physics concepts in their everyday work," says Phil Bucur, the ninth-grade engineering teacher. When, as occasionally happens, some models fall apart on the table, the engineers assure students that it's all part of the design process, and the students return to their blueprints for the next attempt.

In all of these experiences, students are not only building rudimentary professional networks, but are learning *how* to network, and also why networking is so valuable. Day by day, they're also getting practice in how to conduct themselves in a professional environment. One student told us how his own behavior gradually changed after several days of lunching at the GE Lighting corporate cafeteria. "Everybody else is in suits and ties," he said. "It kind of calms us down. We kind of conformed to the place and became more calm and focused. Walking around the campus, you feel an air of importance because you're here in this environment, a Fortune 500 company. You have to be professional."

In fact, MC^2 has so skillfully leveraged its real-world partnerships that its three campuses are frequently visited by science celebrities, who almost always make time to talk with the students. In recent years, these have included NASA chief scientist Waleed Abdalati and Segway inventor Dean Kamen.

Andrea Lane, a recent MC^2 graduate, connected the dots for us as to how these experiences improved her academic progress. "In an average school, you just study for a test and that's it," she said. "But at MC^2, you're excited to retain the information because you're always reciting it back, and you have no idea who's going to be there listening—it could be a company CEO."

A DIP IN THE LABOR POOL

As a freshman at the Science Leadership Academy, Tyler Morales was keenly interested in astronomy, but he was having a hard time coming up with an idea for a project for the science fair that year. That's when his dad used their membership to the Franklin Institute and took him to the museum to hear the chief astronomer, Derrick Pitts, give a talk. Morales approached Pitts after his presentation to ask for advice, impressing Pitts with his initiative. Pitts continued the conversation in several subsequent meetings, and ultimately recruited Morales as an intern to help him in his research. Morales's main job was to capture live images cataloging surface activity on the sun and process them with sophisticated software.

Over the next three years, Morales recruited a group of other SLA students who shared his passion for astronomy, and turned

his assignment first into an intensive two-year internship—
working six to eight hours a week alongside the adult staff of
the institute's observatory—and eventually into the focus for
his senior project. The pictures he took contributed to Pitts's
research and were also featured on the institute's website. The
Franklin Institute has since turned Morales's project into a formal program at the school, called Project Space. Morales told
us that he was recruiting freshmen and sophomores so that he
would be sure it would continue after he graduated.

Morales's story illustrates not only the extraordinarily rich
resources of schools that strategically affiliate with research institutions, businesses, and nonprofits, but a common attitude
among the most innovative schools about the role of student internships. At most U.S. high schools, whether or not a student
has an internship—and also whether that internship is anything other than a glorified gofer kind of job—usually depends
on the ingenuity of that student's parents, and the contacts the
family can tap. In contrast, at the schools we visited, internships were a major part of the high school experience, were genuine learning experiences, and in most cases were mandatory.

Traditional secondary schools in the United States focus
solely on academic achievement and classroom practice, while
only a small percentage focus on developing students' social
capital both inside and outside of school. Schools in predominantly low-income areas therefore need to help students learn
how to connect and work with individuals inside and outside
of the school in order to generate their awareness of the various life and career opportunities that exist and to learn how to
network. Jeff McClellan, principal of MC^2, values getting his
students, who are all from an urban area, out of their local environment. McClellan believes it is the responsibility of him

and his teachers to get the students interested in a path that will lead them to a job. "We want them to have skills, interests, and motivation to be successful whatever path they go. Our job is to just help connect them with that and others."

The teachers and principals running these schools share the conviction that to cultivate Deeper Learning skills, it's essential to expose kids as early as possible to what the world of work is like. They also believe that high schoolers can rise to the high expectations of the working world. Again and again, their students prove them right.

These convictions are one more reason that smart school leaders seek out and maintain strong relationships with professional institutions of all kinds. "We have set up a false dichotomy with work on one side and school on other," says High Tech High principal Larry Rosenstock. "The bandwidth is much broader if we work together."

There is research to support the value of these apprenticeships in terms of student engagement and achievement, and even on their earnings later in life.[9] In a 2006 survey of high school dropouts, 81 percent said they would have been more likely to graduate if schools had provided opportunities for real-world learning.[10] Moreover, graduates of high schools that established firm links between school and getting a good job earned 11 percent more per year, on average, eight years after graduating than students from conventional schools.[11]

As with Morales's work at the Franklin Institute, the internships we witnessed at the schools we visited were all opportunities to do genuinely creative, collaborative, and meaningful work right alongside veteran employees. We learned of high school interns who have designed software to operate an automated pizza machine at Rockwell International, who have reported on sports for the *Philadelphia Inquirer*, and who have tested the elements that go inside the filaments of lamps at General Electric, among other challenging, real-world tasks.

Deeper Learning schools cultivate skills vital to modern work demands and do so to such a degree that employers are routinely impressed by the sophistication of their student interns and how rapidly they adapt to their responsibilities. The bosses soon realize they don't have to worry about how the kids will fit in with a professional culture or whether they will show up on time. Most of them have already been thoroughly exposed to the adult world of work and are ready to take the initiative in their internships, whether that entails meeting deadlines, problem solving, or working in teams.

At MC^2, where internships during eleventh grade are both required and eligible for academic credit, several students were some of the first high school kids from the city of Cleveland to be accepted to work at major local technology companies. One of the MC^2 interns at Rockwell who worked on the pizza-maker software program—a "design-challenge" task that lasted six weeks and included an assignment to develop and present a marketing strategy for the new product—said, "It wasn't hard for us to do this because it was just like our sophomore project."

An internship experience is fundamental to help connect and ground the Deeper Learning that students are engaged in, and all of the schools we visited require at least one before graduation. Casco Bay High School maintains a database of sites where students have had successful placements, including the Portland Conservatory of Music, the local television station, a chemistry and biology laboratory at the University of New England, and even a local bakery.

In San Diego, meanwhile, High Tech High has devised a particularly well-planned internship program. Over the years, it has evolved into a semester-long experience with more than six hundred potential work-site placements. Juniors must complete 140 hours at an intern site to receive credit toward graduation. "We discovered that if you want a bona fide internship program that is central to your school, it can't just be this little program on the side," Rosenstock told us.

The school's staff has worked hard to make sure that the sponsoring internship organizations, including for-profit and nonprofit organizations, offer students meaningful experiences that link back to what they've learned in school, and encompass opportunities for problem solving, collaboration, self-direction, and communication. In pursuit of this end, Rosenstock also switched responsibility for coordinating the internships from a single staff member to the high school's humanities teachers, on the assumption that they would be in a position to know their students better, customizing their work and keeping track of their progress. Each fall semester, the teachers help students plan for their internship, including writing a resume, putting together work samples, setting up interviews, and even practicing for the first meetings with their prospective employers. Then, early each spring, the teachers visit potential internship sites. In April, one month prior to the internship, designated supervisors from the host organization come to the High Tech High campus to learn about the kinds of projects students typically do at school and to gain appreciation of the importance of the internship project. These supervisors must agree to monitor the interns at work and provide feedback to their teachers. They also commit to completing a performance review at the end of the internship and to participating in a program called Coffee Talk, in which interns interview the mentors about their careers. Each intern, furthermore, must prepare a year-end presentation about their experience for an audience of sophomore students, to help them start thinking about what kind of position they might seek.

Often an internship will help ignite a student's smoldering interest in a profession, as it did for Jenn Wright. As a junior at the Science Leadership Academy, she learned that the *Philadelphia Inquirer* offered student internships, although at the time they were supposedly limited to college students. Wright asked her school's internship coordinator to help her write a letter of appeal to the paper's sports editor, and was thrilled, if also a little nervous, when she was invited to apply. During the interview, Wright offered to answer phones at the paper as a way to get her foot in the door, but was delighted when the editor asked her instead to blog about high school sports for the paper's website. In no time, Wright was reporting once a week after school to the newsroom, where she sat next to the newspaper's full-time sports reporters as she cranked out her blogs. She told us that she realized that journalism had a lot in common with the inquiry and research methods she was already learning at SLA, adding, "You have to learn to interpret so many different things, talk to so many different people. You have to pull information together from so many sources." Wright said she also learned how to conduct herself as a professional. "The amount of e-mails I have to send to schedule interviews is incredible," she noted. "When I send an e-mail I think, 'How would I respond if I received an e-mail like this?' It's really important to be polite, to ask for things in a way that people would want to help you."

During the course of the internship, Wright summoned her nerve once again to approach the *Inquirer*'s education writer, whom she convinced to be her mentor. She went on to petition her teachers at SLA to start a journalism class, which in short time was producing its own newspaper, with Wright as its news editor.

WHAT'S IN IT FOR THE PARTNERS AND COMMUNITIES?

It's rare, of course, for anyone to do anything for purely altruistic reasons, and so it is to varying extents with these partnerships. While GE Lighting and NASA volunteers may donate hours of their time for the personal satisfaction of seeing young people thrive, leaders of corporations and even museums are normally obliged to weigh the potential pros and cons of what, in the case of MC^2 and SLA in particular, are enormous contributions of money and employee time. In these cases, they've clearly concluded that embracing these schools is a good investment, for many reasons.

GE Lighting, for instance, has been reasonably concerned about the future quality and quantity of labor in its headquarters' city. The graduation rate for the Cleveland Metropolitan School District had declined from 62 percent in 2006–7 to 53.7 percent in 2007–8, the year before MC^2 opened its doors.[12] (In the 2011–12 year, only 56 percent of the district's students graduated high school on time, compared with 95 percent from MC^2.) The average ACT test score that year was a 16, far below the standard score of 20 for work force readiness.[13] "Even more than just educated workers, we need innovators and those who take on challenges and develop solutions in this project-based world," Andrea Timan, GE Lighting's MC^2 liaison, told us. The lighting business is changing faster than at any time in the last century, she said, adding, "And it will continue that way. We need strong individuals who can keep us ahead of the game."

Throughout the United States, similar concern by business leaders has in recent years fueled the greatest surge of private support for public STEM specialty schools since the 1950s Cold War space race. The fear is that America is losing ground to foreign competitors whose schools are in better shape than ours, particularly when it comes to science and engineering. The National Research Council warned in 2011 that "more than half of the tremendous growth in per capita income in the 20th century can be accounted for by U.S. advances in science and technology," yet many experts fear we're resting on those laurels, at our peril. While there are varied opinions and perspectives on how the economy has shifted and what exactly that means for work now and in the future, very few disagree with the fact that the general landscape, and what is and will be required of our kids, has indeed changed.

As worries over the state of the future work force have grown, some savvy high school principals have begun working with corporate officials to design curricula specifically to interest students in the available jobs. Allan Weiner, principal of Grover Cleveland Charter High School in Reseda, California, told *Education World* that his school had created academies based on the "needs of society in the next 20 years," adding, "I think the best way to get industries and businesses interested in your school is to have courses that support those industries. Advertise that fact and they will come seeking you."[14] Grover

Cleveland High's academies include a manufacturing school focused on metalworking skills sought by hundreds of local firms, who are now sending representatives to the school to work with students. Weiner has also cultivated partnerships with big local firms like Boeing and Sony and attracted interest from several nearby hospitals by opening a new academy dedicated to health service careers.

GE Lighting's extraordinary "embedded partnership" with MC^2 is echoed in a broader effort by the GE Foundation, based in Fairfield, Connecticut, in collaboration with seven school districts in the states of Ohio, Georgia, Pennsylvania, Kentucky, Wisconsin, New York, and Connecticut. Part of this effort involves support for disseminating the new Common Core curriculum. We should note that while similar, the foundation's efforts are distinct and separate from the programs and partnerships developed by the corporation. GE Lighting has also begun a paid internship program with MC^2—a first for the corporation—that by 2013 had placed fifteen students in temporary jobs. Although no graduates had yet been hired permanently when we spoke with Timan, she had high hopes that at least some of the internships would lead to full-time jobs.)

NASA officials who work with MC^2 share GE Lighting's concern about raising the number of students trained in science, math, and engineering. "We are all aware of aerospace and national security needs," Carolyn Hoover, education specialist for NASA, told us, adding that when the NASA staff first heard about the potential partnership with MC^2, "We got really excited. . . . We hope this leads to a healthier northeast Ohio economy and a dynamic work force as well." NASA scientists make routine presentations to incoming MC^2

freshmen about the benefits of STEM careers. And sometimes, the students themselves become STEM ambassadors.

On the SLA website, a student named Matthew Ginnetti
described his capstone project as one of educating underclass-
men in astronomy by leading mini courses for the ninth graders, together with mentors including the Franklin Institute's
chief astronomer Derrick Pitts. Ginnetti has also created a
prototype application for the Franklin Institute to educate users about the International Space Station. "The lack of astronomy interest and education within the United States is
primarily why I chose this project," he wrote.

Apart from their long-term interests in ensuring a future
labor supply, leaders of for-profit and nonprofit organizations
alike understand that partnering with schools improves their
community standing, including with customers and donors.
Great Lakes Science Center, for instance, has applied for
grants in conjunction with MC^2. As Whitney Owens, vice
president of education for the museum, put it: "We leverage
all of our relationships with MC^2. We benefit from the halo
effect of a great school."

Finally, corporations and community groups that support
their schools often discover that individual students return
the favor in a variety of unusual ways. Just as the embedded partnerships we've described are so much more influential than conventional school-business relationships, the kids'
contributions to these extraordinary partnerships also end
up as more lasting and meaningful, further deepening their
schools' ties with the community, in a virtuous cycle.

In Portland, Maine, for instance, seventh graders and their
teachers at King Middle School worked with professionals
from the City of Portland and the Gulf of Maine Research

Institute to contribute to the city's efforts to identify and remove invasive plant species that have become epidemic. Recently, the school kids helped prepare a set of cards, downloadable from GMRI's website, featuring pictures and descriptions of the invasive plants.

In Philadelphia, SLA students have similarly contributed their brainpower and energy toward making their city more sustainable, in this case by conducting a recycling audit of their partner, the Franklin Institute. In St. Paul, Minnesota, students from the Avalon School created a Mobile Community Garden in front of their campus, situated in a gritty, industrial, urban neighborhood. The students worked with their teachers and a local artist to develop public art, including a sculpture the kids built with bicycle parts, and to extend the garden near the new light-rail tracks. The sculpture, which also serves as a mobile garden bed, has sides that depict dragons, the school mascot, and mosaics the students created in their art class. As the exhibit outgrew the space outside the school, the kids moved their plants and art onto the neighborhood's main thoroughfare, University Boulevard, beautifying the neighborhood and extending a friendly calling card to their community.

THE ART OF STRONG NETWORKS

Increasingly, there is support on all sides for strong public-private partnerships that benefit student learning and public education.[15] In several cases, business groups have catalyzed creative school partnerships. In San Diego, with High Tech High, as in Cleveland, with MC^2, local corporate leaders provided an impetus to create a new public school, which then enjoyed above-average business support. No matter how much help the schools receive from politicians or corporate heads, however, principals and teachers at schools with extraordinary partnerships must often extend themselves in unconventional ways.

Active partnerships like those described in this chapter require school staff members to behave like entrepreneurs, in some cases seeking out opportunities by tapping their social and professional contacts. "We're not hiring any new teachers who only know their classes' content," said Carrie Bakken, a founding teacher at the Avalon School. "The teachers have to know how to network." In many communities, this means that teachers and principals alike write letters, make phone calls, and attend meetings of business councils, such as the Rotary or Kiwanis clubs or the local chamber of commerce, to scout out partners.

Since teachers are often frontline managers of the partnerships, they are critical to the equation, employing their social and management skills to nurture and maintain the relationships. Some schools, such as Cedar Heights Junior High School, in Port Orchard, Washington, even provide teachers with special training in navigating these relationships.[16]

One teacher who has risen to this challenge is Steve Payne, who teaches science at King Middle School and orchestrates the seventh graders' contributions to the invasive species program year after year. Payne has been the point man between the school, city, and GMRI, working repeatedly with many of the same people, who together have agreed to speed past bureaucratic obstacles to make sure the students' real-world forays are not just safe but meaningful.

When schools partner with corporations—a trend that's still mostly quite new—both sides need to pay extra attention to avoid conflicts of interest and controversies. The worlds of government-funded education and for-profit business aren't naturally harmonious, and all kinds of misunderstandings can arise. An example, according to one MC^2 teacher, is GE Lighting's continuing practice of giving the tenth graders on its campus an intellectual-property nondisclosure agreement and a stipulation that any inventions created would be owned by the corporation. "Most of the parents don't know what to do with these things, so they just don't hand them in," the teacher said. "GE Lighting had originally tried to say that the kids whose families didn't sign them wouldn't be able to attend, but they eventually had to drop that." Andrea Timan, the community relations manager, confirmed in an e-mail that the confidentiality agreement practice continues as part of the lease agreement with the school district, adding that GE Lighting tracks the submissions and if the forms aren't signed, they risk violating the school's lease agreement. These sorts of information and knowledge gaps can arise in the managing of partnerships, and they are important to address so that everyone involved—students, parents, teachers, and industry professionals—can feel informed, supported, and empowered to get the very best out of any collaboration.

What hardly needs to be spelled out is that teachers involved in such partnerships need time in their schedules for all the networking, relationship nurturing, potential controversy managing, and project coordinating involved. Our model schools all recognize this and provide them that flexibility, formally and informally. At Casco Bay High School, for instance, the school's guidance counselor, who is also in charge of developing partnerships for the district, spends eight hours a week developing relationships with local organizations solely to identify potential sites and hosts for internships. At the same time, the heavy use of technology and emphasis on students working independently at all of the eight schools we visited naturally allows teachers more time to spend on reaching outside the classroom.

Right from the start, building strong community networks will also always depend on strong leadership, both at the schools and at their corporate and community partners. Over the past decade, for instance, SLA's principal Chris Lehmann has determinedly built up his celebrity-educator cred, blogging, tweeting, and giving animated talks, including a 2011 TEDx speech, as he promulgates his inspirational vision of public education transformed along the lines of the Science Leadership Academy. Lehmann's notion of a school without constraining walls extends far beyond the idea of kids taking classes at the Franklin Institute. SLA's yearly "dis-orientation" ritual has students roaming in teams through downtown Philadelphia, recording observations about the city library and train station and public park, which they will then produce as reports and theatrical skits. The message: the world offers endless opportunities for learning.

For both SLA and MC^2, which have the most extensive partnerships of the eight schools we visited, the alliances have helped the schools weather hard times. SLA was able to remain optimistic and even expand despite $1 billion in budget cuts and six different superintendents in the past seven years, while MC^2 weathered budget crackdowns that included layoffs of 80 percent of its staff in its first year.

As Lehmann told us, his school's partnership with a community anchor has made all the difference in expanding his school's national footprint. "The Franklin Institute occupies such an important place in the mental space of Philadelphians that to have them as a partner immediately lent us a legitimacy," he said. In 2011, shortly after our visit to SLA, the White House honored Lehmann as a Champion of Change. In June of 2013, the academy opened a middle school five miles away from its founding site. Naturally, it will also be a partner of the city's cherished science museum. "Without the Franklin," says Lehmann, "this doesn't happen."

A BLUEPRINT FOR DEEPER LEARNING

- Reaching beyond classroom walls as a part of providing students with integrated learning challenges is a game-changer for envisioning, creating, and supporting Deeper Learning experiences.

- Teachers must constantly shift roles: in addition to taking on curriculum design, advising, and coaching, they become networkers who scout opportunities for their students. In doing so, they model many of the skills the students themselves ultimately acquire through the valuable institutional partnerships.

- Tapping local resources—including museums, corporations, academic institutions, nonprofit organizations, and other groups—to form substantive collaborations that engage students meaningfully brings Deeper Learning to life. These experiences make education much more relevant, exciting, and engaging, while motivating kids and helping them explore potential career paths.

- Meaningful alliances provide mentors and social networks that otherwise might not be available to students and can be key to their lifelong success.

- As another means of pulling students into the work of learning, these connections often support improved academic performance among students, including increases in graduation rates.

- Strong partnerships between schools, businesses, and community organizations build a shared sense of responsibility for the success of both the students and the communities to which they belong.

- Creating such partnerships takes vision, time, energy, and leadership from everyone involved, at both the personal and institutional levels.

5

INSPIRE

CUSTOMIZE LEARNING TO MOTIVATE EACH STUDENT

> "Each kid has to have their fuse lit for that rocket to take off." —Gary Allen, GE physicist and volunteer at MC² STEM High School

FROM EDGY TO ENGAGED

Andrea Lane first suspected that high school might not be so terrible a few days before classes began. The first inkling came on the afternoon of the egg drop.

It was during a series of exercises at the MC² STEM High School in Cleveland to welcome and prepare incoming freshmen—one of those necessary dis-orientation activities. The new students were assigned to teams and given just fifteen minutes to design a parachute for an egg, using a Ziploc bag, string, cotton, and toothpicks. Each team would then release its egg from the top of a second-floor stairwell. The team that managed to avoid cracking its egg won the honor of having created the best design.

Lane's team's egg cracked. She was energized just the same.

"*Everybody was working together, even though we didn't know each other at all—we'd just met,*" *she recalls.*

Lane hadn't flourished in school before arriving at MC². She was gifted in math but temperamentally restless, chatty, and distracted—a losing proposition in traditional "sit and listen" classrooms. She finished assignments before anyone else and then couldn't stand to be idle. Frequently bored, she talked out of turn, and challenged her teachers whenever she thought they were wrong, which was fairly often, and which, she says, made them defensive.

"*I was always being pulled out of class and sent to the principal's office,*" *Lane remembers.*

In middle school, she got Bs and Cs, and was a loner, she says, because "people would think I was a show-off. It's just that I always knew the stuff and I didn't like to waste time."

Lane's mother, who recognized both her daughter's gifts and her frustration from not being challenged by her middle school, dreamed of sending her to a private high school. With six children, however, Lane's parents were already hard-pressed financially, and Lane didn't want to be a burden. That's why she decided, on her own, to check out MC² STEM High School, even though she was initially skeptical that she would fit well in any classroom at all.

She remained skeptical for the first few weeks after the egg drop—and then she met Brian McCalla.

McCalla wasn't your run-of-the-mill high school physics teacher. He holds two bachelor's degrees, three master's degrees, and a doctorate. Several years earlier, at thirty-four, he had been earning a mid-six-figure salary as he shuttled back and forth to Asia, developing advanced energy-efficiency projects for buildings as a vice president for Johnson Controls, a Fortune 500 firm. He was in Beijing when he got a long-distance call from his doctor back in Cleveland. McCalla had a brain tumor, and he was facing an eighteen-hour surgery.

After his recovery, McCalla amazed his former colleagues by returning to school yet again—this time to prepare for a job teaching high school. "A lot of people thought I'd lost my mind," he says. He believed he'd discovered his calling. In 2007, McCalla became one of the founding teachers at MC². Some of the other instructors also have backgrounds in business, while others have more traditional teaching backgrounds. All share McCalla's enthusiasm about what devoted teachers and talented students can accomplish together.

Lane was in McCalla's first class, and he remembers her vividly. "This school was a perfect fit for Andrea, and she just came barreling through," he recalls. "She was interested in everything, soaking up everything you could give her. She was also assertive as hell. You don't meet many kids like that. To the extent that anyone knows what they want at that point, she did."

Soon after classes began, McCalla recruited Lane to his new physics club, which was already attracting a highly interested group of students. They met every Saturday from 1 to 8 P.M., and on Thursdays from 4 to 9 P.M.

It was on one of those afternoons, as McCalla remembers, that Lane asked him what sort of career path she should follow. He cautiously suggested mechanical engineering. Mechanical engineers, he says, are the jack-of-all-trades of engineering, able to work in many disciplines. And Lane's interests and talents were all over the map.

With McCalla's encouragement of Lane's relentlessly curious brain, she began to see herself in a different light—a key step for students on the path to acquiring an academic mindset. No longer the struggling middle schooler, she could see that not just McCalla but other MC² teachers were recognizing her abilities, working to support her future path to becoming a professional. In tenth grade, she began managing the Fab Lab, the school's sophisticated mobile industrial workshop. As a junior, she traveled to Lima, Peru, to address a global conference on Fab Labs. As a senior, she designed an LED-lit Christmas tree ornament that ended up in the downtown Cleveland holiday decorations. When we caught up with Lane, she was still restless and chatty, switching topics at high speed. Yet she said she never had time for distraction at MC². "You're just always doing something," she said, laughing.

LIGHTING THE FUSE

It took a motivated and mindful teacher in an institutionally supportive context to understand that the problem with Andrea Lane wasn't really a problem with Lane—she simply needed to be appropriately challenged, with consideration of the way she learned best and found meaning in her schoolwork.

"These students need adults with unwavering commitment to them, so we look for teachers who know their content and care about kids—you can't have just one or the other or you won't change lives," says MC² principal Jeff McClellan.

Indeed, it wasn't only McCalla who contributed to Lane's success, but a group of dedicated teachers, and a context that supported them in trying various approaches to bring out the best in their students. (McClellan used to sign his e-mails with the motto, "Whatever it takes.") This goes back to the determined focus of schools dedicated to Deeper Learning on building exceptional communities, in which high academic expectations are clearly conveyed. Particularly helpful in this regard is the common practice of having students work both independently and in groups, giving teachers the time and flexibility to get to know them as individuals.

A truism about teenagers—one that actually seems to be true—is that they'll rarely be open with adults when surrounded by their peers. Such honesty is even rarer in the top-down context of most high schools, and especially when the teens in question have been struggling in school, with their confidence often sapped. Yet when students are able to meet individually with teachers, in the course of working as members of groups or on individual projects, they more readily see that teacher as a supportive resource rather than simply another judgmental adult. This allows students opportunities to reveal themselves more fully, while their teachers can help them develop their talents.

It's at these informal, unstructured moments, said McCalla, that students "show you things that you would never be able to see just from their course work. That's when you really get to figure out who they are, to understand their personalities and their lives outside of school, and also to gain their trust."

The ensuing conversations can help teachers discover student interests and connect them with fitting opportunities, such as the way McCalla recruited Lane to the physics club. More subtly, as he noted, better knowledge of the students' everyday lives can also help teachers tailor approaches to the kids' emotional states. "When they're frightened, you want to encourage them, and when they're proud, you want to support them," McCalla said.

From his off-the-cuff conversations with Lane, McCalla learned, among other things, that she was the youngest of six high-achieving students and eager to join the competition. "It's mostly her sweat that gets her where she goes," he said. "She really responds to a challenge." The insight inspired him to encourage Lane to carve out her own expertise, develop her strengths through progressively more difficult tasks, and ultimately become more confident.

In recent years, cognitive scientists have offered strong evidence to support such tactics, suggesting that learning can be more profound and lasting when teachers develop strong relationships with students, while also tailoring experiences as much as possible to their differing motivations, strengths, and limitations.[1] Education professor Kurt Fischer, chairman of Harvard University's Mind, Brain and Education program, says that schools that ignore the dramatic variability of their students as a result end up failing as many as 80 percent of them.[2]

In contrast, teachers at the schools we visited were constantly looking for "hooks" to motivate their students, helping them discover and pursue their interests and take up the reins of their own education. That's how Andrea Lane ended up in Lima, working with three other students, from Chicago, Kenya, and Amsterdam, on a project to design a chair as part of the international conference on Fab Labs. Meanwhile, as we've previously mentioned, Jenn Wright, a student from the Science Leadership Academy, was covering sports for the *Philadelphia Inquirer*. Around the same time, Eliza Unger, then a junior at the Avalon School, was surging ahead in her schoolwork, even after discontinuing her medication for attention deficit/hyperactivity disorder (ADHD), while her classmate, Holly Marsh, got a paid job as a ranger for the National Park Service, and Justin Ehringhaus, a previously introverted junior at Casco Bay High School, was studying Japanese—in Japan.

In each of these cases, and in so many others like them, teachers discovered different ways to hook the teens into pursuing their educational passions. Sometimes, it was as simple as a single, encouraging conversation. Sometimes it took finding the right internship or mentor. The point, as so many thoughtful teachers know, is that students, like most people, behave differently in different contexts, and, above all, depending on whether they are authentically engaged and experiencing some control and success. That's how today's distracting class clown becomes tomorrow's Robin Williams, today's dyslexic dropout becomes tomorrow's Sir Richard Branson, and today's under-challenged, economically disadvantaged kid becomes tomorrow's Ursula Burns.

"Each kid has to have their fuse lit for that rocket to take off," Gary Allen, a GE Lighting physicist who has volunteered at MC^2 for the past two years, said in an interview with Edutopia.org. "You can get them out on the launching pad, but if you don't light that fuse, they're not going to go."[3]

UNTANGLING THE CORD

Discovering the key to motivate each student obliges teachers to be flexible as they constantly shift strategies. At one moment, they'll be designing and adjusting curriculum; at another, they'll be scouting opportunities outside of the classroom, and at yet another, they'll be acting as a sports coach of sorts, weighing teens' strengths and interests, plotting a course for students to make the most of themselves, and, not least, cheering from the sidelines.

"Brian McCalla was my engineering teacher who became my math, science and, any-other-type-of-help-I-needed teacher, and he has been my mentor ever since," recalled Andrea Lane. "He always pushed me to do more and was never satisfied, no matter how big the project was. He didn't limit my thinking because I was a certain age or grade, but opened my mind to think out of the box and more abstractly. The day he gave me my personal wireless soldering iron was the day I knew I could make anything I set my mind to."

McCalla's mentoring helped Lane develop the academic mindset that University of Chicago education researcher Camille Farrington describes as a factor in acquiring perseverance (i.e., grit) and a critical component to the acquisition of Deeper Learning skills. "The more perseverance a student exhibits, the more likely he or she is to attend class even when other things interfere, to complete homework even when it is challenging, and to continue pursuing academic goals even when setbacks or obstacles get in the way," Farrington writes.[4]

From McCalla's description, when Lane arrived at MC[2], she was a student who had no shortage of drive. Yet researchers have found that many struggling African American students like Lane, as well as other students of color facing academic challenges, benefit greatly from specific approaches aimed at helping them see themselves as learners. Research by Harvard University economist Ronald F. Ferguson suggests that to best support the success of minority students, teachers need to "inspire the trust, elicit the cooperation, stimulate the ambition and support the sustained industriousness" of students who, for a host of reasons, aren't reaching their potential.[5]

One student almost missed her chance to develop an academic mindset in high school, although she plainly has it today, as an enthusiastic senior-year student at Avalon. The student's vivid metaphor for what high school was like for her first two-and-a-half years is a pair of headphones with a cord tangled in knots (by which she means the schools) and earbuds (by which she means herself) that didn't fit the cord. As a freshman at a conventional, lecture-based public high school, she doodled in her notebooks instead of taking notes. Failure there led her to a small but rigorous charter school, where she quickly fell behind, as she described it, "drowning in late assignments." Her parents switched her to a third school, home-based and online, with hopes that the flexibility might help. But the student floundered without structure and failed nearly every class. By her junior year, she had been diagnosed with ADHD, anxiety, and depression. She came to fear that she would never graduate. "There was something wrong with me. I couldn't learn. I couldn't absorb and retain the information," she told us. "The headphone cord was hopelessly looped in a million different ways and the earbuds lost somewhere in the mess."

That's when the student's relentless parents convinced her to try one more school, which turned out to be Avalon. There, she met teacher and school leader Carrie Bakken, who helped her pursue a new approach to her education, which Avalon teachers refer to as "student-initiated learning." The student was given various options for how to pursue her studies, including that instead of taking six seminars a day, she could pick how many classes she would take or take none at all, and instead design her own projects. The student got to work, at first reluctantly, and then enthusiastically, engaging in a school routine she came to think of as "the perfect concoction of structured independence."

For her first independent project, she drew a diagram of the brain, labeling all of its parts and explaining to an audience of teachers what each part did. In developing the project, she not only had to make sure it was of high quality, but that it aligned with state science standards. Her teachers, who were grading her from a rubric, told her she had met both objectives, which meant she could receive her needed biology credits. She felt as if the headphone cords were finally beginning to untangle.

As they do with all of their students, the Avalon teachers took care to understand the student's particular mix of strengths and challenges, calling attention to the strengths while helping her cope with and face the challenges. After learning of her diagnoses, for instance, they drew up a plan that gave her permission to take breaks from class when she was feeling overwhelmed to go study in the cafeteria. While many traditional schools have formal arrangements— hammered out in committees—for Individualized Education Programs as mandated by federal law, the Avalon teachers put the student in the driver's seat, inviting her to tell them what she needed in order to take more responsibility for her own education.

The student began her senior year, in the fall of 2013, excited about embarking on several new projects. Her perseverance has been fueled by a series of novel successes to the point where she has become a public advocate for schools like Avalon. In December of 2012, she was invited to speak as a member of a panel at the national conference of the Council of State Governments in Austin, Texas. There, she told her story to policy makers from throughout the United States. As she told us, the support she got at Avalon to take more control of her own education, "saved my confidence, my high school career, and my future."

Sometimes all it takes to put a student on the path to achieving an academic mindset is to link him or her up with an adult who shares a passion. That's how Avalon counselor Kevin Ward successfully advised a senior student who he felt seemed disengaged with school. The student shared his own assessment with us directly as well via a recent e-mail exchange. "I was in a different world than others," he wrote. "I considered myself very weird and I attempted to avoid possible embarrassment within the classroom and in my personal life."

As the student's advisor, however, Ward also knew he was keenly interested in military history—his sophomore project had been based on the book *On War*, by Carl von Clausewitz—and that his interest opened the door for him to experience academic success. So Ward introduced the senior to the father of an Avalon graduate who designed geological survey maps for the state of Minnesota. The map-maker worked with the student on his senior project, focused on the Battle of Gettysburg. As the student recalled, that connection was a "major shift" for his project, as he was "forced to become interested" in map-making after he realized what an effective tool a good map would be in his eventual presentation to his class. Making maps made the student feel as if the battles were coming to life. The expert helped him find a free online map-making program, troubleshooting problems with him along the way, and then paid for the student's map to be printed out in a professional style.

The student ended up delivering what Ward described as an "informative and thoughtful" presentation, the best work he had done in school to date. The student agreed. "The senior project was something I was in love with," he wrote from his dorm at Northwestern University, where he had enrolled in the fall of 2013, with plans to major in history. "That is probably why it seemed I was more energetic as a student in my senior year." Now an alumnus, he added that the project was "pivotal to my academic path," improving his critical thinking while deepening his appreciation of military history. "I am currently using my skills in map-reading and understanding a general's mind to the biggest advantage I can muster," he wrote.

NO NEED FOR COOKIE CUTTERS

Quite often the most immediate way to light a student's fuse is to make sure he or she can connect what teachers are teaching to what's happening in the real world. This was the case for Holly Marsh, a senior at the Avalon School. Marsh, as mentioned previously, got a paid job as a national park ranger on her sixteenth birthday in December of 2009, an achievement she credits in large part to her seventh-grade life science teacher, who hooked her with a class on ecology. As a ninth grader, Marsh began volunteering with the National Park Service Volunteers in Parks program, monitoring part of the seventy-two-mile portion of the Mississippi River that runs through the Twin Cities. The following year, Marsh persuaded her advisors at school to turn that volunteer work into an unpaid internship, for which she got academic credit. She logged more than three hundred hours, mostly on Saturdays at the visitor center, where she guided camping and canoe trips, created hundreds of buttons for various programs, and occasionally dressed up, in a full-body, bright-green costume, as Freddie the Flathead Catfish, the mascot for the Mississippi National River and Recreation Area. Back at school, Marsh gave talks to teachers and peers about the Park Service and the Mississippi River, and wrote a series of reflection papers on her experience. Early in Marsh's junior year in high school, the superintendent of the recreation area invited her into his office, surprising her with his offer of a federal job as a "visitor use assistant."

In 2010, Marsh won the George B. Hartzog Jr. Award for the Park Service Youth Volunteer of the Year, given each year to honor outstanding volunteers across the National Park Service. She and her parents were flown to Washington, DC, for a banquet ceremony attended by the president of the National Parks Foundation.

Marsh told us that Avalon had set her on her career path, and that after graduation, she intended to continue working for the National Park Service, to pay for college. She has become such an appreciative champion of her school that as her senior project, she worked with a local policy institute to support new legislation in Minnesota to promote "Individualized Learning Schools."

Were it not for Avalon, Marsh has written in an essay for her school, "I would have no doubt been forced to choose between pursuing my passion and boosting my transcript in order to look appealing to four-year institutions. In other words,

I would have become another cookie-cutter product of the American school system."

THE POWER OF DUAL ENROLLMENT

Many schools that construct their philosophy around Deeper Learning outcomes shepherd high school students toward the expanded options of higher education as a way to both customize learning experiences—offering otherwise unavailable classes—and to prepare students for their college careers.

Unlike in traditional high schools, where only a few high achievers are permitted to take college classes, all of the students at the schools we visited are routinely and strongly encouraged to enroll at nearby colleges, take college-level classes online, or even take college courses offered on-site at their school. Such "dual enrollment" programs, by which students can simultaneously earn high school and college credits, not only deepen students' knowledge, but strengthen higher-order thinking skills such as critical thinking and analysis.

College courses in Japanese were key in lighting the fuse for Justin Ehringhaus, whom we interviewed by Skype during his senior year at Casco Bay High School while he was studying at a high school in Kumamoto, in the Kyushu region of southern Japan. Ehringhaus described himself as a "passive and disengaged" learner in his first year at Casco Bay, until he discovered a passion for Asian culture and languages after reading James Clavell's novel *Shogun*. What came next was one of those magical mentoring moments. At one of the student-led teacher-parent conferences during Ehringhaus's sophomore year, his crew advisor, a humanities teacher named

Joe Grady, praised his academic performance but questioned why he wasn't involved in other school-based or community activities. "At that time, I just didn't know what I wanted to do or what I was particularly interested in," Ehringhaus said. Grady suggested that Ehringhaus join the Model United Nations program, and he encouraged him to meet with the school's team coordinator. Ehringhaus wasn't a natural joiner, but, buoyed by Grady's encouragement, took the risk—and enjoyed the experience. And in time, much like Andrea Lane, he came to see himself differently. He eventually shed his self-image as a timid loner who "never liked talking to people," in favor of a person "willing to explore the unexplored." An academic mindset was emerging.

Encouraging Ehringhaus's new perception of his own potential, his teachers and principal encouraged and helped arrange for him to take Japanese classes at the University of Southern Maine, where he could take up to six credits per semester for free. Similarly, they helped him obtain an internship at the Council on International Educational Exchange, an international student exchange organization based in Portland, after which Ehringhaus embarked on a six-week study program in three different cities in China via a full scholarship through a U.S. State Department–sponsored summer exchange program. Ehringhaus finally got himself to Japan in his senior year. When we caught up with him once again, in 2013, he was a sophomore at Bowdoin College in Brunswick, Maine, focusing on Asian studies.

In recent years, dual enrollment programs have proliferated among U.S. public high schools, as several states have supported them, on evidence-based grounds. Research suggests the strategy is boosting the rates of both high school graduation and college enrollment. One major study, involving more than thirty thousand students who graduated from Texas high schools in 2004, found that those who took college courses were more than twice as likely to attend and graduate from college than peers who did not. These benefits held for all racial groups and for students from low-income families.[6]

Dual enrollment helps students develop more positive attitudes toward learning (i.e., an academic mindset) by encouraging them to pursue their interests in greater depth than would be possible in high school, while also getting a head start on a college degree. An additional important benefit for students from families with great financial barriers is that tuition is often free of charge, subsidized by state governments and the colleges themselves.

While dual enrollment at the MC^2 high school in Cleveland sometimes begins as early as ninth grade, it is a common option for juniors and seniors. In the 2011–12 school year, 40 percent of the juniors and half of the seniors at MC^2 were enrolled full time and part time in colleges, including Cleveland State, Cuyahoga Community College, Case Western Reserve, and Lorain Community College.

In his role as a networking mentor, one he often takes on for his students, MC^2 principal Jeff McClellan personally advocated for a student named Manuel Martinez, the talented, American-born son of Guatemalan immigrants, who was eager to take engineering courses at Cleveland State.[7] McClellan helped Martinez arrange to meet with an engineering professor at the college, who was initially skeptical about whether a high schooler could handle the course work. However, the professor ended up so impressed by Martinez's abilities that he invited him to enroll in one of his higher-level classes. Martinez went on to take several advanced engineering classes, blazing a trail for others to follow, while also completing an internship with Rockwell Automation. He graduated MC^2 as valedictorian of his class, and he enrolled at Cornell University's College of Engineering on a full scholarship in 2012.

In rural Indiana, Rochester High School has doggedly pursued dual enrollment programs for its students, despite being located inconveniently far from any higher education institution. In 2012, thanks to the school's creative partnerships with three different colleges, about eighty-eight kids, or 17 percent of Rochester's student body, were taking a college course for dual credit. Ivy Technical Community College lets Rochester students take classes online or at a nearby satellite campus free of charge. In a separate arrangement, both Indiana University and Ball State University, each of which are located about two to four hours by car or bus from Rochester, offer courses in subjects including English composition, Spanish, and calculus, taught by university teachers who travel to the high school campus. For portions of the Ball State courses, students watch videos of the college professors while supervised by the Rochester teachers who have been certified by the university. "Through dual enrollment, I got to see what the workload is like and feel prepared to handle college," said one Rochester student, who was taking fourteen college credits in her senior year.

When high school students are set free to explore higher education, they often surprise their teachers with both their interests and their enthusiasm. One junior student at the Avalon School took the initiative to find a course on Ojibwa, a rare Native American language, being offered at the University of Minnesota. "I practice every night before I go to sleep," she told us. "I go over vocabulary. . . . I count in my head. Spanish classes are great, but when you get to choose a language, it's far more meaningful. . . . It's like: I *get to learn this* instead of *I have to do this*."

For her senior project at SLA, a math whiz named Luna Frank-Fischer, who'd been inspired by advanced courses at the University of Pennsylvania, developed a website, Luna's Math Help, offering resources for students struggling in math, in which kids can find help according to and organized by their preferences—e.g., videos versus graphs—as well as by topics.

START WITH THE END IN MIND

With their teachers' consistently high expectations always in mind, and with clear, customized support along their path to becoming independent learners, students again and again impressed us with what they were able to achieve. Freed from traditional educational systems that expected and relied on their passivity, many of them naturally progressed to taking on surprisingly mature kinds of challenges that tested their capacities for critical thinking, collaboration, creativity, and communication.

Andrea Lane, for instance, recalls a trip she made to Ohio's state capital in Columbus during her sophomore year, as part of a delegation from MC² to rally lawmakers' support for STEM schools. In an example of the power of high expectations, Andrea Timan, the GE Lighting liaison, had asked Lane to write and deliver a speech, which Lane remembers as "the scariest thing I had to do as a fifteen-year-old girl. I walked onstage and my heart dropped. This was epic to me because if I messed up, then they could think negative things about our school and I didn't want that responsibility. But after all those emotions, it was successful, and once I started talking I got into the zone and got a standing ovation."

Timan described Lane as "so creative, driven, and energetic that I will, and do, ask her to be on my team whenever I can. Andrea is a trustworthy individual who has already proven herself as a great project leader, and I won't be surprised when she calls to tell me that she has opened her off-the-grid restaurant where she has grown all of the products on top of the rooftop of that restaurant or has just become the CEO of a business."

Brian McCalla, Lane's first mentor at MC², enthusiastically shares that perspective. When last we spoke with him, he was helping her look into scholarships as she made plans to enroll at the University of Pittsburgh. His pride in her accomplishments, and in watching so many other students who'd flourished from a tailored approach to inspiring students, was why, he said, "I'll never, ever, ever leave this profession. I don't have children myself. But I know how a proud parent feels."

A BLUEPRINT FOR DEEPER LEARNING

- Finding the spark—a subject, idea, or project that makes a student light up—is the key to customizing learning experiences for individual students.

- In order to tailor learning to meet individual students' educational needs and aspirations, teachers should seek out and develop a balanced knowledge of each student's unique tendencies, circumstances, and interests through both formal (performance, observations) and informal (casual conversations, insight from parents or other teachers) means.

- Effective ways to align learning with a student's interests and strengths include external partnerships and mentors, tailoring course work (e.g., independent, specialized projects), and dual enrollment in available postsecondary offerings.

6

WIRE

MAKE TECHNOLOGY THE SERVANT, NOT THE MASTER

"Technology needs to be like oxygen—ubiquitous, necessary, and invisible."[1]—Chris Lehmann, principal of the Science Leadership Academy

ALL THE NEWS THAT'S FIT TO TWEET

Rochester High School science teacher Amy Blackburn is thrilled, for the most part, by her students' ample access to information technology. The school provides a laptop to every youth it serves, and Blackburn feels certain that the world of information at her students' fingertips spurs their progress toward becoming independent, deeper learners. "When they ask me a question that I have no clue about, I tell them to look it up," she says. "There is so much more information out there than a textbook or a teacher could ever have. They need to learn to go get it."

With her freshmen, especially, Blackburn spends a lot of time teaching students how to search for information on the Internet. She comes up with engaging ways to do this, such as sending kids

on scavenger hunts in which the goal is to find specific websites related to a topic they are studying. And each year, she also makes sure to have them check out a website titled "Ban Dihydrogen Monoxide!"[2] There, the students read about the dangers of "an invisible killer," routinely dumped into rivers and streams, which is "colorless, odorless, tasteless, and kills uncounted thousands of people every year." The site warns that symptoms of ingestion can include "excessive sweating and urination, and possibly a bloated feeling, nausea, vomiting and body electrolyte imbalance," while, "for those who have become dependent, DHMO withdrawal means certain death." The website is the work of Donald Simanek, a mischievous emeritus physics professor. And, of course, it's a hoax.

As Blackburn explains, "[Some] students get the point immediately, but all of the students eventually realize that the website is describing water. That moment provides me the opportunity to do a lesson on how to evaluate what you find on the Net."

REALITY BYTES

As schools throughout America race to wire their classrooms—buying laptops, tablets, and software galore—Deeper Learning schools in general, and particularly the ones we visited, are well ahead of most in reaping the best advantages that modern technology can offer, from expanding research opportunities, to facilitating teacher-student communication, to helping students take more responsibility for their own learning. This happens in several ways, among them using programs and applications that build students' writing skills, offer digital methods to design projects, and broaden students' options for presenting work creatively. "Technology needs to be like oxygen—ubiquitous, necessary, and invisible. It's gotta be part and parcel of everything we do,"[3] Science Leadership Academy's principal, Chris Lehmann, is fond of saying. Lehmann, together with so many other teachers we interviewed, appreciates the power of technology to help students develop and strengthen their self-direction, critical thinking, communication, and collaboration through a range of applications. Still, as Blackburn's cautionary tale about dihydrogen monoxide (aka H_2O) shows, educators need to remind their students to continue to think critically in evaluating whether these important new tools are enhancing or interfering with their learning.

The digital transformation of education seems inevitable as schools strive to catch up to the rapidly changing world outside their walls. In 2011–12, more than 2.5 million public school students took at least one online course, compared to just 750,000 five years earlier. Sixty-five percent of schools reported that they had a "digital-content strategy." And nearly 70 percent of educators said they wanted more e-learning tools than they already had. Additionally, more than 70 percent of teachers said that they think technology in the classroom helps them do their jobs better, by engaging students' attention, reinforcing and expanding content, and accommodating different learning styles.[4]

The inexorable changes underway are happening on all fronts. For example, onscreen assessments related to the new Common Core State Standards are currently in development and will be field-tested in 2014. (They are slated to be rolled out in 2015.) The plan is for tests to no longer be printed, as in decades past, on paper multiple-choice forms. In pilot tests given to more than 1 million New York students in 2013, kids responded to questions and prompts on computers—wielding mice to drag, drop, and highlight—while utilizing the basic tech skills essential in today's world.

Schools that take on a Deeper Learning ethos are well prepared for this challenge, as they eagerly embrace all sorts of technology and thoroughly integrate it into their students' days. Their teachers accept that innovative technologies are most certainly here to stay and realize that they don't *have to be* a distraction. Thus, you'll rarely see students lugging textbooks through the halls of Casco Bay High School, King Middle School, Impact Academy, or High Tech High, among others. Instead, kids are nimbly managing all kinds of new technology—communicating with each other through e-mail and social media; writing away on desktops, laptops, and tablets; creating unique projects with tools including iMovie, Flash, Flickr, and mashups; and conducting sophisticated research in technology-based facilities such as High Tech High's advanced biotechnology and robotics labs and MC²'s MIT Fab Lab.

READY, SET, CLICK

Familiarizing students with computers and software early on is an important step to integrating technology effectively and smartly. The Science Leadership Academy, among several of the schools we visited, requires ninth graders to take a class on computer basics, from which they move on to learning how to operate a variety of programs that they will use to increase the efficiency of their work process to support their learning—

from creating presentation slides and writing research papers to modifying images and sketching product designs.

Teachers also focus on the personal implications of the digital age, and what students will need to know to navigate a rapidly transforming society. For example, Marcie Hull, SLA's technology czar, instructs students on how best to establish and maintain their digital identities. "I try to model how to bring yourself out on the Internet," said Hull, who herself pops up on Pinterest, Facebook, Google+, Google Images searches, and LinkedIn. "It helps to have teachers who have a digital persona," Hull said, adding students need to ask themselves "Who am I digitally?" "I tell them to Google me. They have to learn that nothing is private anymore. Everyone is starting to have a digital lifestyle."

The embrace of technology includes a great deal of pragmatism about its potential downsides. Teachers said they acknowledge directly to students that at times students can't avoid being distracted, while offering guidance about how to manage the distractions. "We can't expect kids to be on task every minute of the day," said Hull. More often, of course, on campuses throughout America, it's adults who need to hustle to catch up with students, who've been living the digital lifestyle for years, as they Skype, blog, surf, and skip from video games to virtual worlds.

"Digital native" students,[5] born in the fast-changing 1990s and having grown up with rapidly evolving technology, have come to expect computers to be a part of their lives, including in school. Even so, hundreds of thousands of teachers at traditional schools are still struggling to figure out how to make technology a valuable tool in the classroom, rather than an aimless supplement.[6] In contrast, as we visited Deeper

Learning schools, we found both teachers and students manipulating cutting-edge tools that in both subtle and obvious ways boost kids' academic progress while preparing them for the high-tech world and work force.

At its best, information technology can go far to support each of the main Deeper Learning strategies we've illustrated in this book, from facilitating collaboration, to supporting active, project-based learning, to adding relevancy and reaching out beyond classroom walls, to helping teachers tailor learning experiences to each student.

COLLABORATIVE COMMUNITIES THAT RESEARCH, REFLECT, AND REVISE

At Rochester High, science teacher Amy Blackburn has her students use a suite of options, including e-mail, discussion forums, Google Docs, and Google Sites to communicate with each other in real-time on projects. Google Docs registers each team member's contributions to a project just as it does in genuine office settings—eliminating the thorny he-said, she-said debates of years past.

Similarly, at the Science Leadership Academy, tenth graders in English teacher Larissa Pahomov's linked English and history class use Wikispaces, a free online educational tool, to create poetry portfolios. Pahomov knows it will be motivating for students, given their enthusiasm for social networking. Students use the program to write their own poems and a forum allows them to edit and comment on each other's writing, and then comment on other students' feedback. Meanwhile, Pahomov can monitor the exchanges and offer extra help only when needed; for instance, if a student seems stalled in his or her writing, or if a critic needs suggestions on how to be more diplomatic. This learning tool helps writing become a more communal process and mirrors something that is also happening more and more on campuses and in professional settings.

Technology has the ability to shift traditional power dynamics in educational settings. At their discretion, teachers can free themselves from constantly being the primary interlocutors. Instead they remain at a distance, monitoring conversations to make sure the feedback is constructive and not hurtful, and stepping in only occasionally as the students learn to take responsibility for their own and each other's progress. More broadly, technology spurs collaboration by creating and strengthening virtual communities that give students and their teachers new ways and different modes of trading ideas and providing feedback.

"Technology creates opportunities to make the work real," says David Grant, the technology integrator at King Middle School. "If you are working in the world today, there's little chance you won't be working on a computer. For anything that is complex, requires an outcome product, needs collaboration, communication, research, etc., there will be software or hardware in the middle. Without this, school is pretend." While other teachers may still ask kids to keep private journals of their reflections in class in notebooks, Grant encourages them to post them online, to "make their thinking visible" and invite other students to respond.

Many Deeper Learning schools rely heavily on student presentations as a means for students to share their work with the school community and to demonstrate their understanding of the academic concepts involved in a project. Rather than just reading aloud a written speech, students are encouraged and often required to create more complex, engaging presentations using PowerPoint, Prezi, and webinars, or even by making a DVD. These schools also encourage students to use the technology many of them already have regular access to, in the form of now less expensive cell phones and digital cameras, for school-related projects. Supporting students to feel like, and behave like, professional documentarians, they can venture out into their communities to conduct all kinds of research and gather material.

Managed strategically, technology can give students novel opportunities to practice reflection and revision, both critical to the Deeper Learning process, by making those pursuits more authentic and engaging. Simply through an ability to save (digitally), track, and time stamp, technology can help students better reflect on and revise their work. Considering how many homework papers get lost in backpack transit between school and home in traditional schools, eliminating that factor is a big deal in itself. Added to this is the advantage that as students build their digital portfolios, they can go back an unlimited number of times to revise what they've done. Naturally, when students can search through their work in one place (as opposed to behind bureaus, under car seats, and hidden by parents in attics), they can also play a more active role in reviewing their own progress over the course of their school career. Essentially, technology allows for work to be archived, which in turn enables more efficient and fruitful reflection and revisions. In this way, Hull says, digital portfolios encourage students to keep asking, "What will I do next time that will make my learning better?"

REACHING OUT TO THE WORLD

No matter where they stood on the spectrum of digital natives to immigrants, the teachers we interviewed agreed that there has been no greater advance in the classroom than the Internet for adding relevancy and immediacy to classroom content.

During the Arab Spring protests in Egypt, in 2011, for instance, Avalon Charter School social studies teacher Gretchen Sage-Martison decided in the middle of a unit on the Middle East to cast aside what was rapidly becoming an outdated textbook in favor of having her students conduct their own online research of media websites and blogs by Middle East experts, as events unfolded. "I can't depend on a textbook when everything is changing in real time," Sage-Martison said.

Today's students have free and immediate access to an unprecedented universe of information, including newspaper articles, maps, photos, real estate records, obituaries, legislation and pending bills, research journals, and, in the best of cases, even collections from research libraries and universities around the world. What this means, among other things, is that when juniors at SLA were studying the journeys of Hernán Cortés, they could locate and read translations of the explorer's journals and copies of letters that had been written to him, as well as scholarly articles, papers, and book reviews. Another class, studying the contemporary debate about immigration reform, could go online to read texts of strict new immigration laws in Alabama and Arizona, and compare them to nineteenth- and twentieth-century responses to earlier waves of newcomers.

In all sorts of ways, new technologies help students reach far outside their classrooms. For a project on the 2008 elections, a class from SLA partnered with a group of students in Texas to put together a contrasting picture of Election Day in their two states. The two groups captured the sights and sounds of the election with cell phones and digital cameras, and then collaborated, using photo sharing and instant messaging programs, to produce their report.

BOOTING UP RESPONSIBLY

One digital trend quickly catching on throughout America's public and private schools involves a cottage industry of learning management systems, also known as course management systems or virtual learning environments. These online systems represent a watershed in education, since they encourage independence, contributing to students becoming more responsible for their own learning by helping them organize their work, track their progress, stay on task, and communicate more quickly and directly with their teachers.

All of the schools we visited relied on learning management systems in one form or another. In each school, students have developed the habit of signing on to the system at the start of each class to see what is scheduled for the day—much as, in other classrooms, students glance at the chalkboard in front of the room—and then refer to the site periodically throughout the day as they work on their projects.

One of the most powerful images at Rochester High School was the daily routing of the students and teachers at the beginning of class. Students immediately log into the learning management system, where everything the student needs to progress through their current project and everything the teacher needs to review each student's progress exists, including the project objectives, assessment rubrics, content resources (the name of the textbook, online text, or videos), sample products, class schedules, and deadlines.

Like many other teachers, Amy Blackburn at Rochester High finds that when students are able to spend at least some class time working independently on their computers, it frees her up to teach more efficiently, as she circulates around the room advising groups on projects and being able to take more time to help students who are struggling. "What I most like about our school is how fluid the classroom is," she says. "Students are on the computers, they function in groups, and I am just guiding their work."

Moreover, these systems can offer important tools that ensure equal access for students with varied learning styles or distinct learning challenges to engage subject material critically and have Deeper Learning experiences. For example, by presenting content in different ways, say via graphs and videos for the more visually inclined, by translating passages for English learners, or by sounding aloud words for kids who have dyslexia, teachers are supported in their efforts to bring meaningful learning to each and every student.[7]

To support project-based learning, Rochester High School uses a tool called Echo, which was designed by the New Tech Network, a collection of schools that serve as models for Deeper Learning. Echo encompasses a long list of features, including instant messaging, online chat groups, student journals, and peer feedback tools, in addition to a library of resources that includes instructional videos on using various software programs, a community directory, and a suite of communication and publishing tools, including Gmail, Google Docs, and Google Sites.

SLA uses a somewhat similar system, developed through a customizable program called Moodle, which is a free, open-source platform that reportedly has more than 73 million users in 237 countries. "Moodle is the in-box of our class," Gamal Sherif, a science teacher at SLA, told us. "Students have access to every assignment and resources for their projects."

Within systems such as Echo and Moodle, teachers are also afforded restricted access to systems that allow them to track individual students, from attendance rates and test scores to narrative descriptions of academic progress and behavior. This more efficient mode of information sharing can be invaluable in helping teachers coordinate their efforts to address potential problems and challenges with students, enabling them to do so more thoughtfully, more comprehensively, and as early as possible.

In another variation on the learning management theme, the Avalon School in St. Paul uses a system known as Project Foundry, as do all the other members of Avalon's national school network, EdVisions Schools. Project Foundry's website includes a particularly attractive element for schools in this era of confusion over how best to integrate the requirements of the new Common Core State Standards, suggesting it can help the schools demonstrate that students are meeting their respective state learning standards. One feature, called Brainstorm, includes a form that requires students to think hard about and clearly express a new project's "deliverables," goals, and milestones, and an estimate of the hours it will take to complete each of the milestones. Students must download and complete the form before they can receive faculty approval for a project.

The Brainstorm form not only helps the student clarify his or her thinking, but serves as a basis for a discussion with an advisor before the student hands in a full proposal. Once the advisor approves a plan, another tool, called Project Proposal, lets the student transfer information directly into the school's learning management system. Next, the student completes a "grading rubric," another major support for the goal of creating more self-directed learners. This form requires the student to provide evidence that the project will not only be of high quality, but will align to state standards—in this way transferring a job that had always been up to the teacher to the student, who is now expected to have a deeper understanding of just why he or she is making certain choices about what to learn. The student then meets with the advisor and a teacher responsible for content related to the project to discuss each piece of the planning process. If the two adults give a thumbs-up on the project proposal, the rubric, and a time-management plan, the student then posts the work schedule on the online school calendar, and from then on, uses another system feature to log in the hours spent on the project.

While all of these learning management steps are geared toward putting students in the driver's seat as much as possible, they also make it easier for teachers to monitor and support students' progress on individual and team projects. Teachers are able to focus their questions, asking, for instance, "Where are you on your timeline in relation to what you proposed to accomplish?" or "I see you have already logged in one hundred hours, but you only have five sources listed in your annotated bibliography. How do you plan to expand your research?"

THE WRONG WAY TO WIRE

In a game-changing development toward the end of the first decade of the new millennium, the prices of educational programs and devices finally fell to levels more competitive with textbooks. In 2009, California's then-governor Arnold Schwarzenegger announced that the Golden State would be the first in the nation to switch to e-textbooks. One year later, the federal Department of Education released its National Education Technology Plan, declaring:

> Technology is at the core of virtually every aspect of our daily lives and work, and we must leverage it to provide engaging and powerful learning experiences and content, as well as resources and assessments that measure student achievement in more complete, authentic, and meaningful ways. Technology-based learning and assessment systems will be pivotal in improving student learning and generating data that can be used to continuously improve the education system at all levels.[8]

Even so, three years later, hundreds of thousands of classrooms, including whole districts and states, have missed out on learning opportunities—and even opportunities to cut costs—largely because teachers and principals haven't understood how to effectively harness the power of technology to support student learning.

The eight Deeper Learning schools we visited have much to teach the country in this regard. All have figured out how to use technology to create engaging and meaningful experiences for students. Significantly, the teachers we interviewed were not so enamored of technology that they were blind to the pitfalls, which can include unnecessary distractions in the classroom or an overreliance to the point where the humanizing influence of teachers recedes. For example, valuable people skills, like collaboration and public speaking, are rare and sought-after in the modern work force, and they are a core focus of any Deeper Learning strategy. The development of these abilities often depends almost entirely on skillful modeling and coaching by actual people with solid experience to share with students. As SLA principal Chris Lehmann says: "The purpose of tech should not, cannot ever be, to reduce the number of caring adults in the classroom."

John Naisbitt, in his book *High Tech High Touch: Technology and Our Search for Meaning*, cataloged the dangers of what he calls the Technologically Intoxicated Zone—a state of simultaneous fear and worship of the technology that has already saturated U.S. culture. Naisbitt and his co-authors ask several important questions, including whether technology really saves us time or merely ends up adding to our daily list of tasks.[9]

Most if not all of the teachers we interviewed are, knowingly or not, students of Lev Vygotsky and others who have emphasized the value of interpersonal connections in learning.[10] Their approach to integrating technology incorporates classic research by Albert Mehrabian, suggesting that more than 50 percent of communication is nonverbal, a matter of body language, while much of the rest comes across in the tone of spoken words, leaving only about 7 percent of meaning transmitted by actual words.[11] In other words, they're cognizant of the limits of bits and bytes in the sacred task of transforming young lives.

We continually noticed signs among our example schools

that teachers temper their e-enthusiasm with a hefty helping of good judgment. At High Tech High, for instance, principal Larry Rosenstock rejected a proposal to bring students to campus just one day a week while expecting them to work online from home the other four days, saying he wanted to keep the emphasis on high-quality human relationships.

At Rochester High, we watched Dan McCarthy, the sophomore English teacher, tell his students to put their computers aside for the first few days of a challenging new project on the Industrial Revolution. Instead, he directed them to form into teams, which he provided with paper and markers, instructing them to create flow charts to help them visualize connections between the historical figures they were studying, including such notables as Andrew Carnegie, Jacob Riis, Lucien B. Smith, George Washington Carver, John Deere, and Samuel Gompers. Using the old-fashioned paper system gave the kids time to form into functioning units, with everyone sitting close together and contributing ideas as a group, rather than letting the work get reduced to one person typing on a keyboard, McCarthy explained.

Rochester High science teacher Amy Blackburn told us that she is keeping up her yearly tradition of sending freshmen to look up the website that warns of the supposedly mortal dangers of H_2O. For the sake of students who don't get the point the first time around, Blackburn told us that she follows up later in her course by sending the class to investigate the credibility of dozens of websites, including YouTube videos and online photographs, dedicated to revealing the existence of human male pregnancies.[12]

WIRED FOR DEEPER LEARNING

Recently, the Los Angeles Unified Schools district launched a billion-dollar plan to equip every student and teacher with an iPad. Since the launch, the plan has been mired in challenges to the full rollout, among them concerns about the number necessary and the funding, and discussions about their proper use and what restrictions, if any, should be applied to the school-issued devices.[13] Much of the latter debate has centered around whether students should be allowed to use their devices for purposes that don't fall under certain uses and guidelines set by the district.

While the program in L.A. is still under discussion, and the precise shape it will take has yet to be determined as we write, this particular question is a window onto why technology is so critical to Deeper Learning. It's not that iPads and their use, or any technology integrated into student learning, should be a free-for-all experience. However, imposing a false division between school—and the learning that takes place there—and life does not send the right message to young people if we truly want to encourage the development of learning lifestyles. As with striving toward all Deeper Learning outcomes, the desired results of rules and regulations are often better achieved when those traditional methods are replaced by school norms and setting expectations. Blocking students from using the social networks that keep them current in the digital world does not contribute to learning; but discussing and agreeing on when it's time for Facebook versus when it's time to access their learning management system is the type of thinking that can support real learning.

Like a violin in an orchestra, technology is one instrument—an invaluable one—among many required for a school to engender relevant, meaningful learning. The strategies employed by schools today are the key to making technology work for students and teachers alike. As Chris Lehmann explains, there's a simple way for schools to think about their approach to ed-tech by asking, "What do you what to learn and what is the best way to do that? If tech is not the best way for kids to learn . . . don't force it." While the process of integrating technology can seem overwhelming and confusing, the logic isn't all that different from thinking about how to make use of other tools in the kit. Keith Krueger, the CEO of the Consortium for School Networking, underscores that, "It is important to remember that educational software, like textbooks, is only one tool in the learning process. Neither can be a substitute for well-trained teachers, leadership, and parental involvement."

A BLUEPRINT FOR DEEPER LEARNING

- Technology offers many advantages in educational settings—including expanding research opportunities, improving communication at all levels, and helping students take more responsibility for their own learning—that can help teachers build students' Deeper Learning skills. Computers can be powerful tools for building communities, supporting project-based learning, and reaching out beyond the classroom walls.

- Technology provides new and efficient avenues for students to practice research, reflection, and revision—key strategies for achieving Deeper Learning outcomes. Through tools like online education portfolios, everyone—students, teachers, and parents—can better track and understand students' development over time.

- Technology-based learning management systems can offer students more ownership over their learning experiences and provide teachers, advisors, and administrators with consistent, reliable methods to gauge student progress and determine how best to help.

- Deeper Learning's relationship to technology is defined by enthusiasm mixed with knowledgeable caution, ever mindful of the pitfalls (including distraction, misuse, and overuse) and respectful of the critical role of educators in the classroom.

7

INVEST

DESIGNATE DEEPER LEARNING AS THE NEW NORMAL

"We are currently preparing students for jobs that don't yet exist . . . using technologies that haven't yet been invented . . . in order to solve problems we don't even know are problems yet."—**Richard Riley, former U.S. Secretary of Education**

A BETTER LIFE

It was after dusk and we (Monica R. Martinez and Dennis Mc-Grath) were in Hayward, California, visiting Impact Academy. On this particular night, the school was hosting a special event for families and friends involving demonstrations of a sampling of the school's learning activities. As we sat in the back of the classroom, absorbed in the task of taking notes on the sophomores who were engaged in a Socratic seminar about a novel they'd read, we grew increasingly awestruck by the sophistication of their comments and the thoughtful questions they asked one another. Toward the end of the discussion, we looked up at the parents who were seated around the outside of the students' circle. Most if not all of the parents had come straight from work and were still wearing the customary attire of landscapers, maids, and mechanics. The expressions on their faces were priceless, filled with amazement and pride. Both of us fought back tears as we bore witness to their wide eyes and smiles that seemed to exclaim, "This is my son" and "This is my daughter doing this." The room swelled with a shared feeling that a door was being opened to a much better life for these students. It could not have been more clear that their education was nurturing not just the skills they would need for college, but also a joy for learning that would propel them in ways they had yet to imagine.

The following week, back in Philadelphia at the community college where McGrath teaches, he silently surveyed the faces in his Introduction to Sociology course. The regional center where the class is held primarily serves African American students who come from some of the city's worst-performing schools. Most of the students enrolled are single mothers in their late twenties or early thirties who hope to go into allied health careers. The class discussion that day focused on a research study he had assigned as a refresher on the scientific method. Although the students were engaged in the conversation, they were barely able to demonstrate even a basic understanding of scientific reasoning. It took several attempts to explain variables and hypotheses before it seemed like anything was sinking in.

McGrath, looking at his students, knowing from both professional experience and personal conversations that they desperately wanted well-paying careers to support their children, wondered what their lives today might look like if only they had gone to a school like Impact Academy. College classes like this one would not be the tremendous or even insurmountable struggle that they often are for many of his students; and the better life they aspire to might not seem so distant.

COMING UP SHORT

Shouldn't all young people be afforded experiences like those offered at Impact Academy and the other schools we have profiled? It seems painfully obvious that indeed they should if American ideals of equal opportunity are ever going to amount to more than a hollow promise.

Although we both have served many roles in a range of institutions, we have never been middle school or high school teachers. Perhaps that is one of many reasons we deeply admire how the teachers and principals of the schools we visited engage students in learning so skillfully, and in such a way that is intrinsically motivating to them. As higher education professionals and researchers, we look through a slightly different lens, though we share nearly all of the same considerations that plague our colleagues in the K–12 system. From our vantage point, we have been—and continue to be—deeply concerned with the practices, policies, and initiatives that relate to college access and to every student's ability to complete college successfully. This post–K–12 lens is, in fact, what led us to explore, and to commit to spreading, the ideas, tenets, and outcomes central to Deeper Learning.

Whether in private elite institutions, four-year public universities, or community colleges, we have seen countless students—particularly students from predominantly low-income high schools—come to college uninterested in taking advantage of a place designed to develop the type of curiosity, self-direction, and critical thinking that will preserve and extend their own learning. We have encountered time and time again students who are complacent, who go through the motions—individually and in lockstep—consistently submitting mediocre work.

As a dean at Williams College, Martinez would often hear, "If my professor could just tell me what she wants, I could do that." These are the voices of students primarily concerned with, and possibly fixated on, following directions to please a teacher for a good grade. This is the recording playing in the heads of untold numbers of students, while professors spin their wheels, lamenting the lack of independent, critical thinking and intellectual discourse that students apply to their course work and more generally to their educational lives. Meanwhile, *high school* students at our eight schools are taking on the challenge of maintaining the school's technology; authoring and publishing peer-edited books; creating multimedia documentaries about other communities; testifying to state legislators on environmental issues and educational policy; and helping a city eliminate invasive plants.

At a different point along the postsecondary spectrum, urban community colleges are charged with expanding the minds and skills of students who—to a much greater degree than at your average four-year institution—often walk through the door severely unprepared to reach their academic and professional goals. Equally problematic for these students are the less quantifiable contributors to success, such as social advantages and resources that open up untold opportunities. Recall from chapter four the students at MC^2 who have "buddies" drawn from the professionals who work at the GE International Lighting Division's corporate campus, where the school's tenth-grade courses are located. From the age of fifteen, these students are building social networks that they can draw upon when, for instance, the time comes to apply to college or to look for internships. Often young people who grow up in relatively more affluent families naturally develop or are born into networks that offer this type of information, advice, and assistance. But these networks—the source of something sociologists have termed "social capital"—are generally unavailable to low-income students. That is, if the networks are not intentionally arranged and constructed by those who possess greater social capital themselves. According to Phil Bucur, a teacher at MC^2 STEM High School in Cleveland, principal Jeff McClellan "hires and develops teachers who can connect both with the real world and kids. I am not just a teacher, I am a connection maker. I am . . . the students' window to the world."

Contrast the tenth-grade world that has been strategically designed and cultivated at MC^2—one in which mentors drawn from a group of technology professionals who offer a social network that proves invaluable come time for internships and college applications—to the reality of many community college students or those who never cross even that educational threshold. As a sociologist, McGrath has talked about social capital explicitly with his community college students. It is a completely new topic for them, and the anxiety is palpable as students begin to recognize yet another structural barrier that they face. Once a young African American man inquired earnestly, "I live in North Philadelphia. How can I get one of those networks?" Beyond the lack of social capital, which could provide the opportunities to transform this young man's life, it's troubling, to say the least, that throughout his prior years of schooling no one had ever sat down with him to talk about his dreams, help him form an educational plan to achieve them, or discuss the nature of the civic and professional world that we somehow expect him to participate in successfully.

WHY DEEPER LEARNING IS ESSENTIAL

Recently, McGrath asked a twenty-year-old student to describe what she thought the difference was between memorizing something and understanding it. She had no idea of how the two differed. In a conversation after class, the reason became clear. She had attended some of the worst schools in the city and in these environments was asked to do little beyond memorize facts for tests. She had never been encouraged to do more.

We have taught students in the K–12 education system how to memorize facts through multiple forms of "drill and kill." We've trained them to "get by," to follow the directions and expectations of their teachers. But we have not, en masse, taught them to engage in learning. Therefore, how can we be surprised that only 33 percent of all the students who go on to college are actually prepared for what they encounter? Is it any wonder that so many young people drop out or take six years to earn a degree? Worse yet, only 8 percent of low-income children in America earn a bachelor's degree by their mid-twenties, compared to more than 80 percent of students from the top income quartile.[1]

Taking stock, public education is truly at a crossroads. A system still fundamentally grounded in a nineteenth-century model of organization cannot prepare our students for the twenty-first century. Our world in the current era is certainly more complex than it was when our public education system was established. More important, both the world and the educational preparation needed to live in it have shifted vastly during the past fifty years, around the time when the comprehensive high school model was created and proliferated (as a terminal institution with three tracks).

The traditional way that schools are organized and the form teaching generally takes are increasingly at odds with the cultural shifts produced by the digital age in which students use technology to share ideas, form communities, collaborate, participate, produce, and create—locally, nationally, or globally. If public education does not transform, not only will it become irrelevant, but it will generate more and far-reaching inequality with regard to education and broader life outcomes that have for years been linked to educational attainment.

With so much change and nearly as much opacity regarding what's to come in this century and the next, it's incumbent on all of us to rethink what is needed and valued in our learning, our work, and our lives—a process that should live at the core of our public education system. Now more than ever we need to reignite students' curiosity and instill a hunger for learning by *expecting and empowering* students to achieve more. And that expectation has to go far beyond the rote memorization of facts; it has to embody the development of an academic mindset that enables students to master core academic content, think critically, solve complex problems, work collaboratively, communicate effectively, and be the true leaders of their own learning.

As a nation we have been in a series of wars since 1999, we

have experienced a major economic crisis lasting almost a decade, we have a disappearing middle class, and the top 1 percent of Americans control 40 percent of the nation's wealth. We are in a time when a high school diploma, a valued credential a half-century ago, is not sufficient. Our evolving society demands of people the abilities to comprehend and tackle massive complex problems—such as energy crises, widespread poverty, and climate change—and live with the ambiguity, volatility, and uncertainty of our future. Shaping the future of education in light of these factors will surely require a great deal of innovation, the type of innovation that we have showcased through the powerful examples in *Deeper Learning*. It is our hope that this book will spur more schools to follow suit, because all of our children need and deserve better.

ACKNOWLEDGMENTS

We wish to thank the teachers, principals, and students of the schools we visited. We greatly appreciate how generous they were with their time, but most of all we are grateful for the patience and kindness they showed in letting us observe the wonderful learning environments they create and in helping us understand what Deeper Learning truly looks like in practice. By inviting us into their schools and sharing their experiences, they all became our teachers.

We thank the William and Flora Hewlett Foundation for providing support for our research and the writing of this book. Conversations with Barbara Chow, Marc Chun, Chris Shearer, and Kristi Kimball (now the executive director of the Schwab Foundation) greatly enriched our understanding of Deeper Learning. We would also like to thank our editor, Tara Grove, for her unwavering support of this work.

Finally we thank our partners, Lynne Teismann and Egle Mangum, who had to live with this book as long as we did.

NOTES

INTRODUCTION—HOPE: EIGHT REASONS FOR OPTIMISM ABOUT THE FUTURE OF PUBLIC EDUCATION

1. Philip W. Jackson, *Life in Classrooms* (New York: Holt, Rinehart & Winston, 1968).

2. Thomas Friedman, "How to Get a Job," *New York Times*, May 28, 2013.

3. The description included here mirrors the Deeper Learning principles as outlined by the Alliance for Excellent Education, a group that supports Deeper Learning and advocates for a network of schools, many of them members of new national educational systems such as Big Picture Learning, ConnectEd, EdVisions Schools, Envision Education, Expeditionary Learning, High Tech High, and the New Tech Network. See "About Deeper Learning," http://deeperlearning4all.org/about-deeper-learning.

4. Tom Little, "21st Century and Progressive Education: An Intersection," *International Journal of Progressive Education* 8:3 (2012).

5. Elizabeth Coleman, "A Call to Reinvent Liberal Arts Education," presented at TED Talks, February 2009.

6. Diane Ravitch, *Reign of Error: The Hoax of the Privatization Movement and the Danger to America's Public Schools* (New York: Knopf, 2013).

7. The National Commission on Excellence in Education, "A Nation at Risk: The Imperative for Educational Reform." Washington, DC: U.S. GPO, 1983.

8. Stacy Teicher Khadaroo, "Race to the Top Promises New Era of Standardized Testing," *Christian Science Monitor*, September 2, 2010.

9. Andrea Hacker and Claudia Dreifus, "Who's Minding the Schools?" *New York Times*, June 8, 2013.

10. "What Do We Know about the High School Class of 2013?" Child Trends, June 11, 2013.

11. "College Board: SAT Scores Going Down as GPAs Rise," *Here and Now*, 90.9 WBUR FM, Boston's NPR station, September 26, 2013.

12. "United States," *Education at a Glance 2013: OECD Indicators*, OECD Publishing, 2013.

13. "Are They Really Ready to Work? Employers' Perspectives on the Basic Knowledge and Applied Skills of New Entrants to the 21st Century U.S. Workforce," The Conference Board, Inc., the Partnership for 21st Century Skills, Corporate Voices for Working Families, and the Society for Human Resource Management, 2006.

14. The Editorial Board, "The Trouble with Testing Mania," *New York Times*, July 13, 2013.

15. Amanda Ripley, "What Every Child Can Learn from Kentucky," *Time*, September 30, 2013.

16. Randi Weingarten, "Will States Fail the Common Core?" *Huffington Post*, November 2, 2013.

17. Theodore R. Sizer, *Horace's Compromise: The Dilemma of the American High School* (New York: Houghton Mifflin, 1984).

18. Additional details on our methodology: We conducted two multiday site visits at each of the eight schools. During the site visits, we observed a cross section of classes and interviewed school leaders, teachers, staff, and students, as well as representatives of partner institutions. We returned to several of the schools multiple times and followed up on the site visits with additional telephone and in-person interviews. Our interviews with school leaders addressed the mission and pedagogical approach of the schools. Interviews with teachers focused on their approach to curriculum, pedagogy, instructional strategies, assessment, and support for students, to capture the logic behind their classroom activities. We also collected information on professional development, the extent of collaboration among teachers, and their use of external partners in developing curriculum and providing internships and other learning opportunities for students. We examined a wide range of documents and reports from

the schools, including examples of curricula, projects, and other class-room assignments.

19. National Center for Educational Statistics, "Table 105: Public Secondary Schools, by Grade Span, Average School Size, and State or Jurisdiction: 2009–10," *Digest of Education Statistics: 2011*.

20. Lisa Guernsey and Sonia Harmon, "America's Most Amazing Schools," *Ladies' Home Journal*, August 16, 2010.

21. Tom Loveless, "The Banality of Deeper Learning," Brookings, May 29, 2013, www.brookings.edu/blogs/brown-center-chalkboard/posts/2013/05 /29-deeper-cognitive-learning-loveless.

22. Ken Robinson, "How Schools Kill Creativity" presented at TED Talks, June 2006.

23. Jo Boaler and Megan Staples, "Creating Mathematical Futures through an Equitable Teaching Approach: The Case of Railside School," *Teachers College Record* 110(3): 608–645. See also James W. Pellegrino and Margaret L. Hilton, eds., *Education for Life and Work: Developing Transferable Knowledge and Skills in the 21st Century* (Washington, DC: The National Academies Press, 2012).

1. CONNECT: CREATING A COMMUNITY OF LEARNERS

1. Cori Brewster and Jennifer Railsback, "Building Trusting Relationships for School Improvement: Implications for Principals and Teachers," *By Request*, Northwest Regional Laboratory, September 2003.

2. Anthony S. Bryk, Valerie Lee, and Peter Holland, *Catholic Schools and the Common Good* (Cambridge, MA: Harvard University Press, March 1995).

3. Anthony S. Bryk, "Organizing Schools for Improvement," *Kappan* 91:7 (2010).

4. Linda Darling-Hammond, *Only a Teacher: Teachers Today*, PBS Online, www.pbs.org/onlyateacher/today2.html. Hammond was the founding director of the National Commission on Teaching and America's Future.

5. Camille A. Farrington, "Academic Mindsets as a Critical Component of Deeper Learning," A White Paper Prepared for the William and Flora Hewlett Foundation, April 2013.

6. David Arnold, "Student Goes from Homeless to Harvard University," *NewsNet5*, May 31, 2012.

7.   David Boone, "Heading to Harvard," *Huffington Post*, May 11, 2012.

8.   Jennifer Kahn, "Can Emotional Intelligence Be Taught?" *New York Times*, September 11, 2013.

9.   Abraham H. Maslow, *Motivation and Personality* (New York: Harper & Brothers, 1954).

10. D.S. Hawker and M.J. Boulton. 2000. Twenty years' research on peer victimization and psychosocial maladjustment: A meta-analytic review of cross-sectional studies. *Journal of Child Psychology and Psychiatry and Allied Disciplines* 41, 441–455. See also K. Rigby. 2003. Consequences of bullying in schools. *Canadian Journal of Psychiatry* 48(9): 583–590.

11. G.M. Glew, M. Fan, W. Katon, F.P. Rivara, and M.A. Kernic. 2005. Bullying, psychosocial adjustment, and academic performance in elementary school. *Archives of Pediatric Adolescent Medicine* 159: 1026–1031.

12. Jaana Juvonen, Yueyan Wang, and Guadalupe Espinoza, "Bullying Experiences and Compromised Academic Performance Across Middle School Grades," *Journal of Early Adolescence* 31:152 (2011).

13. Robert Blum, "School Connectedness: Improving the Lives of Students," Johns Hopkins Bloomberg School of Public Health, Baltimore, Maryland, 2005.

14. This is not to imply that bullying and teasing never happen in these environments. Avalon, for example, serves a large number of students who previously struggled in conventional schools. Thirty-two percent are classified as receiving special education—the highest proportion of all of our schools, and more than twice the national average—and many suffer anxiety and depression and struggle with social skills. Whenever possible, the school uses "restorative justice" strategies, bringing kids together to solve minor conflicts themselves. Still, twenty-five students, about 14 percent of the school population, were suspended in 2012–13 for more serious infractions such as fighting or drug use, according to teacher Carrie Bakken. The bottom line, however, is that the community-building efforts appear to be working. Bakken reported that when surveyed, 99 percent of Avalon's students said they felt safe at school.

15. Albert Bandura, *Social Learning Theory* (New York: General Learning Press, 1971).

16. David Grant, *Teacher-Training Coordinator David Grand Describes a Framework for Project Learning Success*, video, directed by Ken Ellis, The

George Lucas Foundation, March 15, 2010, www.edutopia.org/stw-maine
-project-based-learning-authentic-expeditionary-video.

2. EMPOWER: ACTIVATE STUDENTS TO LEAD THEIR OWN LEARNING

1. John Merrow, "An Open Letter to the Architects of the Common Core,"
    Taking Note, May 29, 2013.

2. "Education Secretary Arne Duncan Visits Portland," *News Center*, Portland,
    Maine (August 31, 2010).

3. John Dewey promoted the idea of "learning by doing" in *My Pedagogic
    Creed*, writing: "The teacher is not in the school to impose certain ideas
    or to form certain habits in the child, but is there as a member of the com-
    munity to select the influences which shall affect the child and to assist him
    in properly responding to these." John Dewey, *My Pedagogic Creed* (E.L.
    Kellogg & Co., 1897).

4. *Taking the Lead: An Interview with Larry Rosenstock*, video, produced and
    directed by Ken Ellis, Edutopia, December 3, 2013, www.edutopia.org
    /high-tech-high-larry-rosenstock-video.

5. Research shows that when teachers taught for understanding and mean-
    ing rather than memorization, and when they connected the material to
    students' experiences, their students consistently outperformed students
    in more traditional classrooms on advanced skills and on traditional tests
    (this was elementary age, 140 classrooms, serving disadvantaged kids in
    six school districts). Michael S. Knapp, Patrick M. Shields, and Brenda J.
    Turnbull, *Academic Challenge for the Children of Poverty: The Summary
    Report* (Washington, DC: U.S. Department of Education, Office of
    Planning, Budget, and Evaluation, 1992).

6. Chris Lehmann, "Education is Broken," presented at TEDxPhilly, 2011.

7. James Danckert, "Chronic Boredom May Be a Sign of Poor Health" (origi-
    nally published as "Descent of the Doldrums"), *Scientific American*, July 17,
    2013.

8. John M. Bridgeland, John J. Dilulio Jr., and Karen Burke Morison, *The
    Silent Epidemic: Perspectives of High School Dropouts*, Civic Enterprises in
    association with Peter D. Hart Research Associates for The Bill & Melinda
    Gates Foundation (March 2006).

9. Robert Balfanz and Nettie Legters, "Locating the Dropout Crisis: Which

High Schools Produce the Nation's Dropouts? Where Are They Located? Who Attends Them?" Center for Research on the Education of Students Placed At Risk, Report 70 (September 2004).

10. Caralee Adams, "ACT Report Finds Students' College Readiness Doesn't Meet Aspirations," *Education Week*, April 21, 2013.

11. The 2009 High School Survey of Student Engagement conducted by the Center for Evaluation and Education Policy at Indiana University.

12. Fred M. Newmann & Associates, *Authentic Achievement: Restructuring Schools for Intellectual Quality* (San Francisco: Jossey-Bass, 1996).

13. Judith L. Meece, Eric M. Anderman, and Lynley H. Anderman, "Classroom Goal Structure, Student Motivation, and Academic Achievement," *Annual Review of Psychology* 57 (2006).

14. M.J. Dunkin and B.J. Biddle, *The Study of Teaching* (New York: Holt, Rinehart & Winston, 1974). See also Jere E. Brophy and Thomas L. Good, "Teacher Influences on Student Achievement," *American Psychologist* 41:10 (1986).

15. Research shows that students in project-based learning classrooms get higher scores than students in traditional classrooms. Tali Tal, Joseph S. Krajcik, and Phyllis C. Blumenfeld, "Urban Schools' Teachers Enacting Project-Based Science," *Journal of Research in Science Teaching* 43:7 (2006).

16. "The Quest for Deep Learning and Engagement in Advanced HS Courses," Knowledge in Action, the University of Washington College of Education, the Bellevue Schools Foundation.

17. See, for example, Johannes Strobel and Angela van Barneveld, "When is PBL More Effective? A Meta-synthesis of Meta-analyses Comparing PBL to Conventional Classrooms," *Interdisciplinary Journal of Problem-based Learning* 3:1 (2009).

18. Vanessa Vega, "Research-Based Practices for Engaging Students in STEM Learning," Edutopia, accessed October 31, 2012, www.edutopia.org/stw-college-career-stem-research.

19. Brigid Barron and Linda Darling-Hammond, "How Can We Teach for Meaningful Learning?" *Powerful Learning: What We Know About Teaching for Understanding* (San Francisco: Jossey-Bass, 2008).

20. Howard Gardner, *Extraordinary Minds: Portraits of 4 Exceptional Individuals and an Examination of Our Own Extraordinariness* (New York: Basic Books, 1997).

21. Among relevant research is a forty-year longitudinal survey of 210 resilient

children on the Hawaiian island of Kauai. The researchers discovered this common thread: that all of the resilient children had developed a close early bond with at least one caregiver—not necessarily parents, but sometimes a grandmother, older sister, or other relative in the extended family. See Emily E. Pherner, "High-Risk Children in Young Adulthood: A Longitudinal Study from Birth to 32 Years," *American Journal of Orthopsychiatry* 59:1, 72–81 (1989).

3. CONTEXTUALIZE: TIE SUBJECTS TO EACH OTHER AND KEEP IT REAL

1. Tyler S. Thigpen, "Taking a Relationship-Centered Approach to Education," *Education Week*, September 18, 2013, www.edweek.org/ew/articles /2013/09/11/03thigpen.h33.html.

2. Ibid.

3. Mary Helen Immordino-Yang and Antonio Damasio, "We Feel, Therefore We Learn: The Relevance of Affective and Social Neuroscience to Education," *Mind, Brain, and Education* 1:1 (The International Mind, Brain, and Education Society and Blackwell Publishing, 2007).

4. Interdisciplinary curricula have been shown by several studies to support students' engagement and learning. See Leah Taylor and Jim Parsons, "Improving Student Engagement," *Current Issues in Education* 14:1 (2011). Specifically integrating science with reading comprehension and writing lessons has been shown by several studies to improve students' understanding in both science and English language arts. See, for example, P. David Pearson, Elizabeth Moje, and Cynthia Greenleaf, "Literacy and Science: Each in the Service of the Other," *Science* 328:5977, 459–463 (2010).

5. Linda Darling-Hammond, *Only a Teacher: Teachers Today*, PBS Online, accessed on October 17, 2013, www.pbs.org/onlyateacher/today2.html.

6. Jay McTighe and Grant Wiggins, *Understanding by Design* (Alexandria, VA: ASCD, 2005).

7. Jay McTighe and Grant Wiggins, "From Common Core Standards to Curriculum: Five Big Ideas," *Granted and . . .* (blog), September 19, 2012.

8. Ross Miller, "Greater Expectations to Improve Student Learning," *Greater Expectations National Panel*, Association of American Colleges and Universities, November 2001. See also Jere E. Brophy and Thomas L. Good,

"Teacher Behavior and Student Achievement" in Merlin C. Wittrock, ed., *Handbook of Research on Teaching* (New York: Macmillan, 1986).

9.   Alix Spiegel, "Teachers' Expectations Can Influence How Students Perform," *NPR: Morning Edition*, audio podcast, September 17, 2013.

10. Nicole S. Sorhagen, "Early Teacher Expectations Disproportionately Affect Poor Children's High School Performance," *Journal of Educational Psychology* 105:2, 465–477 (May 2013).

11. Vega, "Research-Based Practice for Engaging Students in STEM Learning."

12. Lowell Horton, "Mastery Learning: Sound in Theory, But . . .," *Educational Leadership* 37:2 (November 1979).

4. REACH: NETWORK BEYOND SCHOOL WALLS

1.   School Report Card, Philadelphia City School District, Science Leadership Academy (Pennsylvania Department of Education Bureau of Assessment and Accountability, 2012).

2.   Sociologists find that social networks have a great impact on school success and job opportunity throughout a child's life. See Alejandro Portes, "Social Capital: Its Origin and Application in Modern Sociology," *Annual Review of Sociology* 24: 1–24 (1998).

3.   Mariko Nobori, "How Successful Careers Begin in School," Edutopia, October 31, 2012, www.edutopia.org/stw-college-career-stem-school.

4.   Farrington, "Academic Mindsets as a Critical Component of Deeper Learning."

5.   John Mangels, "Fabrication Labs Let Student and Adult Inventors Create Products, Solve Problems," *Plain Dealer*, June 18, 2009.

6.   Mariko Nobori, "Tutoring and Mentorship Brings Authentic Learning to MC2 STEM High School," Edutopia, February, 27, 2013, www.edutopia.org/blog/MC2-STEM-high-school-gary-allen-mariko-nobori.

7.   Carla Herrera, David L. DuBois, and Jean Baldwin Grossman, *The Role of Risk: Mentoring Experiences and Outcomes for Youth with Varying Risk Profiles, Executive Summary*. (New York: A Public/Private Ventures project distributed by MDRC, 2013). See also Gayle McGrane, "Building Authentic Relationships with Youth at Risk," *Effective Strategies* (Clemson, SC: National Dropout Prevention Center/Network, 2010).

8.   "John" is a pseudonym.

9. Randy L. Bell, Lesley M. Blair, Barbara A. Crawford, and Norman G. Lederman, "Just Do It? Impact of a Science Apprenticeship Program on High School Students' Understandings of the Nature of Science and Scientific Inquiry," *Journal of Research in Science Teaching* 40:5, 487–509 (May 2003).

10. Bridgeland, Dilulio, and Morrison, *The Silent Epidemic*.

11. Vega, "Research-Based Practices for Engaging Students in STEM Learning."

12. "2008–2009 School Year Report Card," *Cleveland Metropolitan School District, Cuyahoga County*, Ohio Department of Education Archived Reports, 2009.

13. "2011–2012 School Year Report Card," Cleveland Metropolitan School District, Cuyahoga County, Ohio Department of Education Archived Reports, 2012.

14. Laurance E. Anderson, et al. (13 contributors), "School-Business Partnerships That Work: Success Stories from Schools of All Sizes," Education World, www.educationworld.com/a_admin/admin/admin323.shtml.

15. The State Board of Education adopted Ohio's Credit Flex plan in March 2009, allowing for phase-in during the 2009–10 school year. Local school boards, community schools, chartered non-public schools, and providers of career-technical education were required to comply with provisions of the plan by the beginning of the 2010–11 school year. See Ohio Credit Flexibility Design Team, *New Emphasis on Learning: Ohio's Credit Flexibility Plan Shifts the Focus from "Seat Time" to Performance*, Ohio Department of Education.

16. Anderson, "School-Business Partnerships That Work."

5. INSPIRE: CUSTOMIZE LEARNING TO MOTIVATE EACH STUDENT

1. Christina Hinton, Kurt W. Fischer, and Catherine Glennon, "Mind, Brain, and Education," *Students at the Center*, March 2012.

2. Todd Rose and Katherine Ellison, *Square Peg: My Story and What it Means for Raising Innovators, Visionaries, & Out-of-the-Box Thinkers* (New York: Hyperion, 2013).

3. Nobori, "Tutoring and Mentorship Brings Authentic Learning to MC2 STEM High School."

4. Farrington, "Academic Mindsets as a Critical Component of Deeper Learning."

5. Ronald F. Ferguson, "What Doesn't Meet the Eye: Understanding and Addressing Racial Disparities in High-Achieving Suburban Schools," *Policies Issues*, North Central Regional Educational Laboratory, Issue 13, December 2002.

6. Ben Struhl and Joel Vargas, "Taking College Courses in High School: A Strategy for College Readiness," *Jobs for the Future*, October 2012.

7. "Innovative Schools Form Foundation for Education Reform Plan," *Donor Connections*, The Cleveland Foundation, Summer 2012.

6. WIRE: MAKE TECHNOLOGY THE SERVANT, NOT THE MASTER

1. Chris Lehmann, *Chris Lehmann: School Tech Should Be Like Oxygen*. NASSP Convention, February 28, 2009.

2. Donald Simanek, Ban Dihydrogen Monoxide!, www.lhup.edu/~dsimanek/dhmo.htm.

3. Lehmann, *Chris Lehmann*.

4. John Benson, "Technology in the Classroom is Changing Education in America," VOXXI, August 7, 2013, http://voxxi.com/2013/08/07/technology-in-the-classroom-invest.

5. John Palfrey and Urs Gasser, *Born Digital: Understanding the First Generation of Digital Natives* (New York: Basic Books, 2008).

6. Darrel West, "Five Ways Teachers Can Use Technology to Help Students," *Huffington Post*, May 7, 2013.

7. Thomas Hehir, "Policy Foundations of Universal Design for Learning," *A Policy Reader in Universal Design for Learning,* eds. David T. Gordon, Jenna W. Gravel, and Laura A. Schifter (Cambridge, MA: Harvard Education Press, 2009).

8. *Transforming American Education: Learning Powered by Technology*, Washington DC: U.S. Department of Education, Office of Educational Technology, 2010.

9. John Naisbitt, with Nana Naisbitt and Douglas Philips, *High Tech High Touch: Technology and Our Search for Meaning* (New York: Broadway Books, 1999).

10. Louis C. Moll, ed., *Vygotsky and Education: Instructional Implications and Applications of Sociohistorical Psychology* (Cambridge, UK: Cambridge University Press, 1990).

11. Albert Mehrabian, *Nonverbal Communication* (Chicago: Aldine-Atherton, 1972).

12. "A Womb of His Own," Snopes.com, May 9, 2008, www.snopes.com/pregnant/malepreg.asp.

13. Audrey Watters, "Students Are 'Hacking' Their School-Issued iPads: Good for Them," *The Atlantic*, October 2, 2013.

7: INVEST: MAKE DEEPER LEARNING THE NEW NORMAL

1. Sarah Carr, "Getting Real About High School," *Wilson Quarterly*, Summer 2013.

INDEX

familiarizing students with, 164–66
global connections with, 169–70
lessons regarding Internet usage, 161–62
responsibility with, 170–73
strategies around, 177–78
understanding importance of, 174–76
tech squad, 45
Temple University, 95
testing mania, 7
Thigpen, Tyler S., 83
Timan, Andrea, 111, 121, 132, 137, 158
Transitional Presentations of Learning, 76

Understanding by Design (Wiggins, McTighe), 94

Unger, Eliza, 146
University of Chicago, 148
University of Minnesota, 157
University of Southern Maine, 155
US Department of Education, 174

volunteering by students, 19, 152–54
Vygotsky, Lev, 175

Wagner, Tony, 2–3, 7
Ward, Kevin, 35, 151–52
Weiner, Allan, 132–33
Weingarten, Randi, 8
Whalen, Nora, 23–24
Wiggins, Grant, 94
Williams College, 183
Wise, Dan, 64–65
Wright, Jenn, 130–31, 146

PUBLISHING IN THE PUBLIC INTEREST

Thank you for reading this book published by The New Press. The New Press is a nonprofit, public interest publisher. New Press books and authors play a crucial role in sparking conversations about the key political and social issues of our day.

We hope you enjoyed this book and that you will stay in touch with The New Press. Here are a few ways to stay up to date with our books, events, and the issues we cover:

- Sign up at www.thenewpress.com/subscribe to receive updates on New Press authors and issues and to be notified about local events
- Like us on Facebook: www.facebook.com/newpress books
- Follow us on Twitter: www.twitter.com/thenewpress

Please consider buying New Press books for yourself; for friends and family; or to donate to schools, libraries, community centers, prison libraries, and other organizations involved with the issues our authors write about.

The New Press is a 501(c)(3) nonprofit organization. You can also support our work with a tax-deductible gift by visiting www.thenewpress.com/donate.